I0024224

John Campbell Shairp, William Young Sellar

Portraits to Friends

John Campbell Shairp, William Young Sellar

Portraits to Friends

ISBN/EAN: 9783744692700

Printed in Europe, USA, Canada, Australia, Japan

Cover: Foto ©Thomas Meinert / pixelio.de

More available books at **www.hansebooks.com**

WRITINGS OF JOHN CAMPBELL SHAIRP,

PROFESSOR OF POETRY AT OXFORD.

Culture and Religion in some of their Relations. 16mo, red cloth, gilt top, $1.25.

CONTENTS: The Aim of Culture — Its Relation to Religion; The Scientific Theory of Culture; The Literary Theory of Culture; Hindrances to Spiritual Growth; Religion combining Culture with Itself.

Poetic Interpretation of Nature. 16mo, red cloth, gilt top, $1.25.

CONTENTS: The Sources of Poetry; The Poetic Feeling awakened by the World of Nature; Poetic and Scientific Wonder; Will Science put out Poetry? How far Science may modify Poetry; The Mystical Side of Nature; Primeval Imagination working on Nature; Ways in which Poets deal with Nature; Nature in Hebrew Poetry and in Homer; Nature in Lucretius and Virgil; Nature in Chaucer, Shakespeare, and Milton; Return to Nature by Ramsay and Thomson; Nature in Collins, Gray, Goldsmith, Cooper, and Burns; Wordsworth as an Interpreter of Nature.

Studies in Poetry and Philosophy. 16mo, red cloth, gilt top, $1.50.

CONTENTS: Wordsworth; Coleridge; Keble; The Moral Motive Power.

Aspects of Poetry. 16mo, red cloth, gilt top, $1.50.

CONTENTS: The Province of Poetry; Criticism and Creation; The Spiritual Side of Poetry; The Poet a Revealer; Poetic Style in Modern English Poetry; Virgil as a Religious Poet; Scottish Song and Burns; Shelley as a Lyric Poet; The Poetry of the Scottish Highlands — Ossian; Modern Gaelic Bards — Duncan MacIntyre; The Three Yarrows; The White Doe of Rylstone; The Homeric Spirit in Walter Scott; Prose Poets; Thomas Carlyle; Cardinal Newman.

For sale by all Booksellers, or sent, post-paid, on receipt of price.

HOUGHTON, MIFFLIN AND COMPANY, BOSTON, MASS.

J . C . S H A I R P

PORTRAITS OF FRIENDS

BY

JOHN CAMPBELL SHAIRP

AUTHOR OF "CULTURE AND RELIGION"

WITH A SKETCH OF PRINCIPAL SHAIRP
BY WILLIAM YOUNG SELLARS AND
AN ETCHED PORTRAIT

BOSTON AND NEW YORK
HOUGHTON, MIFFLIN AND COMPANY
The Riverside Press, Cambridge
1889

Copyright, 1889,
By HOUGHTON, MIFFLIN & CO.

All rights reserved.

The Riverside Press, Cambridge, Mass., U. S. A.
Electrotyped and Printed by H. O. Houghton & Co.

PREFACE.

THE title of the memorial volume, *Principal Shairp and his Friends*, which Professor William Knight prepared for publication in 1888, indicates the strong element of friendliness which entered into Shairp's intellectual life. From boyhood till death he was a lover of men, and the subjects which he discussed in literature and philosophy constantly appealed to him in their personal relations. It was both his good fortune and his native openness which made him conversant with Englishmen and Scotchmen who in their day and generation affected the thought of their fellows, and his writings bear frequent testimony to the intimacy of his acquaintance with these men of mark. Besides the more or

less formal work of this nature which he
published in his books, Principal Shairp
contributed to biographies by other hands
interesting reminiscences and character
sketches, and it has been thought desirable
to collect some of these into a single, con-
venient volume, since otherwise they would
be likely to escape the knowledge of that
growing circle of readers which has been
formed by the successive publication in the
United States of Principal Shairp's general
writings.

Professor Knight's volume must remain
as a repository for such of Shairp's letters
and for such testimonies from his friends
as the special student of his life will wish;
but its design is likely to exclude it from
a very wide circulation in America. The
interesting paper of reminiscences, therefore, contributed to it by Professor William
Young Sellars is reproduced here as a personal portrait of Shairp fitly introductory
to those Portraits of Friends which Shairp
himself has drawn. It should be said, in

justice to Professor Sellars, that the sketch
as printed in Professor Knight's volume is
given, not continuously, but in sections, according to the period treated; in bringing
these parts together, therefore, some connecting passage may possibly be lacking.
It should be borne in mind, also, that Professor Sellars, though writing for publication, addressed his reminiscences in familiar
form to Professor Knight. The following
summary of Shairp's career will place the
reader in possession of the main facts in
the uneventful life of a scholar.

John Campbell Shairp was born at Hous-
toun, Linlithgowshire, Scotland, 30 July,
1819. His father, Major Norman Shairp,
is described as "a characteristic example of
the old Scottish laird of a past generation;
a man of clear mind, strong sense, and spot-
less integrity of character; proud of his ancestry and his patrimonial inheritance, —
a keen fox-hunter, a strong conservative, a
warm friend. During the eleven years in

which he served in the Indian army he took part in thirteen pitched battles; and during the memorable campaigns of 1803– 1806 he was with his regiment under canvas, exposed to all the trials of an Indian climate. He retired somewhat early from active service; but continued, for more than half a century, to lead the life of an honored country gentleman."

When ten years of age Shairp was sent as a pupil to the Edinburgh Academy. With the interruption of a year of study at home, he remained at the academy till 1834, and then spent another year in special study at Edinburgh. It was at this time, when he was sixteen or seventeen years of age, that he first came to know Wordsworth's poetry, which had a strong influence upon his mind, and on the course of his intellectual and moral life. He had already tried his own hand at verse, and his work after this was strongly affected by his great master.

From Edinburgh he went in 1836 to

the University of Glasgow, where he laid the foundation of life-long friendships with Norman Macleod and others. In 1840 he gained the Snell Exhibition from Glasgow University to Balliol College, Oxford, and matriculated in June of that year, with the intention at that time of taking orders in the Church of England. He resided at Oxford in a momentous period of English thought, and the results of his companionship are easily discoverable in the papers which he afterward wrote and collected in his *Studies in Poetry and Philosophy*.

In the autumn of 1846 he accepted a mastership at Rugby under Dr. Tait, and remained in that position for eleven years. He made an attempt in 1852 to secure an appointment to the chair of Moral Philosophy in Edinburgh, but failed. In 1853 he married, and in 1857 became an assistant to the Professor of Latin in the College of St. Salvator and St. Leonard, St. Andrews, Scotland. In 1861 he succeeded to the Professor's chair, though he had long done

the full work of the office. In 1868, on
the death of Principal Forbes, he was appointed principal, and held the position until his death.   In 1877, also, he was elected
Professor of Poetry in the University of
Oxford, the duties of the office being confined to the delivery of a few lectures.

His literary work, published originally
for the most part in magazines and reviews,
has been collected into the volumes, *Culture
and Religion, Studies in Poetry and Philosophy, Poetic Interpretation of Nature,
Aspects of Poetry*, and *Burns* in *English
Men of Letters.*   These books, together
with his editorial work in the *Life of Principal Forbes*, were published in his life-
time, and his posthumous writings include
Sketches in History and Poetry, and a
volume of *Poems.* He died at Ormsary,
Argyll, 18 September, 1885.

CONTENTS.

JOHN CAMPBELL SHAIRP.

By WILLIAM YOUNG SELLARS.

I FEEL how difficult it is to convey to
those who did not know him any adequate
impression of the fresh and buoyant spring
of life which never failed our old friend and
colleague during the forty years of my intimacy with him ; of the frank natural enthusiasm, tempered but not abated as he grew
older, with which he spoke on all subjects
which interested him ; of his affection for
his friends ; and, generally, of a nature
singularly pure, genuine, and generous, and
a character loyal, reverent, disinterested,
and consistent, from his earliest youth till
his latest years. I feel it also difficult to
select, out of the long period during which
I knew him, those recollections and impressions which might be thought most characteristic of him. I will try to recall my
earlier impressions, and to give an account,
drawn chiefly from what I have heard from

himself, of the influences which formed him
during the time of his education, and also
of his work as professor during those pleasant years when we were colleagues together
at St. Andrews.   I must leave you to select
from these notes what may seem to you
most suitable for the object which all his
friends who take any part in this commem-
oration of him must have in view, — to give
to those who did not know him some idea
of a life as true, beautiful, and, in its own
sphere, as influential for good, as any ever
known to us.

My memories of him go so far back as
the year 1834, when he left the Edinburgh
Academy.   I cannot remember his appear-
ence then; and as I was only in the second
while he was in the seventh class, it is very
likely that I may never have spoken to him.
But I remember in the prize-list of the year
his name at the end of a poem in Latin hex-
ameters, which I read long afterwards, and
which showed, for one so young as he was at
the time, good scholarship and good taste.
I mention this because, when I once spoke
to him about it, he told me that the one part
of his work which he liked at school was the
writing of Latin verses, which, under our

old rector, Archdeacon Williams, was, if
not made so much of (to the exclusion of
other subjects) as in the old English public
schools, still sufficiently encouraged to give
scope for the taste of those who had an
aptitude for it.

Shairp had a just appreciation of the
sound scholarly training and the fresh intellectual stimulus which we got from the
teaching of our rector. Yet he did not
speak with much enthusiasm about his
school-days. He never at any time cared
about school-games, which, though they did
not then play so important a part in school-
life as they do now, must always form a
large ingredient in its pleasure, and are the
chief bond of that companionship which men
like to recall in after years. He cared still
less for, in fact he always disliked and condemned, the strenuous competition which
was the principal motive to work. He
admitted the necessity of applying this motive, at least in the earlier stages of education, but he thought the desire of "beat-
ing" somebody else neither a very elevated
nor a Christian principle of action ; and he
desired to see it give place as soon as possible to a sense of duty, and a sense of pleasure in the work done for its own sake.

The year of his boyhood which he liked
most to dwell on was the year immediately
preceding his last year at the Edinburgh
Academy, when, for some reason or other,
he was kept at home with a tutor. The
love of his home was through all his life
one of the strongest sentiments in his nature, — the sentiment by which more, I
think, than by any other, the successive
stages of his life were — as they were in
him to a degree beyond what I have ever
known in any other man —

"Bound each to each by natural piety."

He always spoke of the influence of a
happy home as among the most beneficent
of the forces which mould character ; and
when in after days at Oxford he saw among
his friends and contemporaries some who
had evidently suffered much from the speculative perplexities which were then in the
air, and by which he himself was for a time
not absolutely unaffected, he seemed to attribute his own comparative immunity from
them to this influence.

One pleasant reminiscence of that year
was, that he then had, if not his initiation
into, yet his fullest enjoyment of, the pleas-
ures of "hunting," which was the one form

of sport for which he thoroughly cared, and
about which, though he had long practically
given it up, he always spoke and wrote
with enthusiasm. One of the most genu-
inely poetical and spirited of his poems,
which I first heard him repeat with an account of the actual circumstances out of
which it arose, in one of our rides together
at Rugby, is " The Run," published, along
with " Kilmahoe," in the first edition of his
poems. The pleasure which he felt in the
sport, and to which he has given a singularly musical expression in that poem, was
not the mere physical pleasure of hard rid-
ing, though he knew what that was, but
the imaginative feeling of the poetry of
the scenes through which it bore him, and
the imaginative outlet which it gave to the
chivalrous and adventurous spirit which he
inherited, and which was conspicuous in his
outward bearing.

The only other pastime into which he entered keenly, and of which also he discussed
and celebrated the poetry, was " curling,"
the attraction of which to him was, partly,
that it was an exclusively national game,
but chiefly, I think, that it was associated
with happy days at his old home in Lin-

lithgowshire, in which some part of his winter holiday was passed every year of his life. If, therefore, his school-life, though it must have had its share in training his intellect, does not seem to have made any deep impression on his character, it was because its influence and any attraction which it might have had for him were overpowered by the strong and kindly influence and attraction of his home. Yet he was thoroughly loyal to his school, and I remember, as I sat beside him, how cordially he entered into the spirit of the jubilee celebration in 1875, over which his friend, the Archbishop of Canterbury, presided, on the completion of the fiftieth year since the foundation of the school, when the older ones among us were reminded of the *actae non alio rege puertiae.*

Of the years passed there [at the University of Glasgow] he used often to speak, and always with unmixed pleasure and enthusiasm. He quoted with sympathy a saying of one of his friends of that time, when he met him in after years, that " he looked back on his Glasgow time as the romance of his life." He had a very cordial feeling to all the professors under whom he

studied, and a grateful recognition of the
good he got from them. He was especially distinguished in the Moral Philosophy Class, and I remember hearing from
the professor on the subject, that his essays
were generally based on Coleridge, whose
teaching was at that time something quite
new in our universities. He has told me
that what made the most powerful impression upon him, among all the lectures that
he listened to, was the inaugural lecture of
Professor Lushington, in the opening of the
session 1838–39. It was a lecture which
not only contained a most just and impres-
sive survey and estimate of Greek literature, but was surcharged with the new
thought and imaginative feeling pervading
the remarkable Cambridge set to which he
belonged, the names of most of whom are
now well known to the world, and some of
whom (and he certainly) looked on Coleridge then as their master, or at least as a
teacher to whom they owed much. Shairp
left the lecture, as he told me, repeating to
himself the line, —

"That strain I heard was of a higher mood;" [1]

[1] He frequently referred to this lecture in the last decade
of his life, and always with the utmost enthusiasm.

and the impression thus produced was confirmed by his attendance on the private Greek class. I can remember his quoting to me at Oxford happy translations of lines or half-lines of Sophocles, and pregnant bits of criticism from the lectures. He gained a prize at the end of the session for an essay on a comparison of the "Ajax" of Sophocles with the "Coriolanus" of Shakespeare, of which the professor, who, though warm in his admiration of merit, was habitually temperate in the expression of praise, spoke in terms of more than common appreciation. The feeling with which they then regarded one another deepened in later life into one of affectionate friendship.

He had great enjoyment in his student-life, and was fortunate in the set of young men among whom he was thrown. During his time in Glasgow, Shairp was, for the only time in his life, a keen political partisan, and was, I think, one of the founders of the Peel Club, which had its origin in the election of Sir Robert Peel as Lord Rector, in the year 1836. He was consistent in after life in adhering to the politics of his youth and early associations; but he never again took an active part in, or cared much about, the contests of parties.

To this time also he referred the beginning of his intellectual life, which, though
expanded and modified by later influences,
flowed consistently till the end in the
channel which his spirit then struck out for
it. Besides the impulse which he derived
from the literary and philosophical classes,
he then first came under the influence of
Wordsworth, which continued, I think, to
be the master influence of his intellectual
life. It required an independent spirit,
and a taste for poetry not learned from
others or adopted from literary fashion,
but αὐτοδίδακτόν, for a young Scotchman in
those days to become an enthusiastic votary
of a poet who was then only known to the
majority of his countrymen by the satire of
Byron, the parody in the "Rejected Addresses," and the criticism of the "Edinburgh Review." The influence of Scott he
had always felt from his childhood, and in
one of the summers during his Glasgow
college days, or in his early Oxford time,
he met Lockhart in a country house, and
had some conversation with him. He used
often to recall his "proud, sad face," as of
one for whom life had no more zest, since
he had lost the companionship of the great

man with whom he was so closely allied.
With these two, Scott and Wordsworth, as
he formed the earliest, so also he maintained the most constant, of all his friendships in the world of letters.

At this time, too, he first felt the stirring
within himself of the impulses and of something of the faculty of a poet. And the
stirring of those impulses and of that faculty were then, as they were through all
his subsequent life, intimately connected
with what was the master passion of his
life, his love of Nature, especially as she
revealed herself to him in long and often
lonely wanderings through the most picturesque scenes in the Highlands and the Bor-
der-country, or among the places which
spoke to him of the more romantic memories of Scottish history. Till his physical
strength began to fail in the last years of
his life, he never missed passing some days
or weeks in these wanderings; and there
were few if any educated men who knew
Scotland, highland and lowland, so well.
He only once, I think, yielded to the almost universal passion or fashion of foreign
travel, and though he got from his summer
abroad a fair knowledge of German for

working purposes, he seemed to regret a summer not passed in Scotland as a summer wasted.

I was only on two occasions with him in his walks, — once in ascending Ben Cruachan in company with the late Dean of Westminster, the present Master of Balliol, his friend Poste of Oriel, and one or two others; and another time, along with one other companion, in crossing the Minch Moor to Innerleithen and back again to Yarrow, the outcome of which walk appeared soon after in one of the most perfect of his lyrical poems, "The Bush aboon Traquair." One could not be with him on such occasions without perceiving how deep and strong and natural was his enjoyment, how eager and exact his observation of every sound and sight that had attraction for him, and with what a vigorous and elastic tread he went over the ground. I was also struck by his resolute determination not to be satisfied till he ascertained the exact spot which he came out to see. A chief source of interest in his poems to those who knew him is that they are the faithful record —

"Of what was passing in that brain and breast"

(to apply to himself a line which he once quoted as applied by some poet of the Lake country to Professor Wilson) in those walks, into which he threw his whole heart and spirit. Although he was entirely different from him in his social temperament, though he had nothing of his exuberant humor, and though he never could, even had he wished it, have filled the same place in the eyes of his contemporaries which the older professor did, and while his enthusiasm was more subdued, and his imagination and taste were, I think, chastened by a finer culture, yet he always seemed to me in his youth to belong essentially to that one among the various types in which the *perfervidum ingenium* of his countrymen manifests itself, of which Professor Wilson was the most eminent representative.

After leaving Glasgow he passed a winter in Edinburgh, before he was appointed to the Snell Exhibition to Balliol. He attended, I think, some of the University classes, but he spoke of that winter as an idle one, given up chiefly to amusement. It was probably, however, not wasted, and may have helped to give him that ease in social intercourse of which young men, almost exclusively college-bred, often painfully feel the want. There was nothing in him at any time of the manner of a mere student or bookish man. He was perfectly at his ease with men of the most diverse tastes and pursuits, — scholars, soldiers, or men of the world, — people of every degree, from that of a shepherd or a plowman to that of those placed at the opposite end of the social scale.

It was in the year 1840 that he was appointed by the Glasgow Professors to a Snell Exhibition to Balliol, and he entered on residence, I think, in the October term. Balliol, though one of the three or four larger colleges, had by no means reached its present dimensions, nor had it the same cosmopolitan character that it has now; but under the judicious régime of Dr. Jenkyns it had gained the same rank that it holds now in university distinctions. The number of men in residence was about seventy or eighty, carefully selected by the master from the best type of public schoolmen, most of them about that time from Eton, Rugby, Harrow, Shrewsbury, etc. The scholars were elected by competition open to all parts of the world, and among those who were contemporary, or nearly contemporary, with Shairp were the "seven," whom he has admirably characterized as they then were, in a poem which appeared some years ago[1] in "Macmillan's Magazine," with the title, "Balliol Scholars." The only survivors of the seven are now the Lord Chief Justice of England and the Bishop of London;[2] but among them all the one of whom his contemporaries had the highest opinion and hopes, as a poet and thinker, was Clough; and I think it was for him more than any of the others that Shairp then felt that idealizing hero-worship which generous young men of imaginative susceptibility feel for the genius

[1] In March, 1873.

[2] Since these recollections were written, two of Shairp's oldest and best friends, who were both scholars of Balliol at that time, and have since been well known in the world, Theodore Walrond and Matthew Arnold, have passed away. To others, as well as to myself, among their surviving friends and contemporaries, this quick succession of losses must have recalled — as much from the distinction of the men as from the bond of almost brotherly affection which united them together, at college and through all their later life — the grand and pathetic lines in which Wordsworth mourns over the quick succession of losses among the best and greatest of his contemporaries: —

> " How fast has brother followed brother
> From sunshine to the sunless land ! "

of their contemporaries. He went one summer with him on a reading-party to Grasmere, and he often talked of its pleasant memories, especially of the delight and amusement which he and all of them had from seeing a great deal of Hartley Coleridge. He told me, too, of his having once, only once, after one of his long walks, seen Wordsworth standing at his garden-gate, and of how he had felt impelled to shake his hand, and to tell him how much he owed to him. But he shrank always from any kind of " lion-hunting," regarding it as rather a form of impudent self-assertion than a reverent tribute to greatness. The seven scholars of his poem were the immediate successors of others as gifted and remarkable, among whom were the late Lord Cardwell, Sir Stafford Northcote, Dean Stanley, and the present master of the college, Professor Jowett, who was one of the younger fellows when Shairp entered on residence, though the great personal and intellectual influence which, as tutor and master of the college, he has exercised over so many generations of pupils did not begin to assert itself till a year or two later. Among the immediate successors of these seven, with all of whom Shairp became intimate, were Archdeacon Palmer, T. Walrond, T. C. Sanders, F. T. Palgrave, the late Professor H. S. Smith, Sir A. Grant, and others.

There was no sharp distinction made between reading and non-reading men, but the whole college formed a very friendly society; and one of the considerations which determined Shairp long afterwards to send his son to Oriel was, that it had not outgrown the size which admitted of a common-family kind of life among its members, of which he himself had felt the charm and benefit at Balliol. Into this society of young Englishmen the Scotch Exhibitioners from Glasgow were heartily welcomed. They brought some prestige with them, for members of their body had added distinction to the college before it had become famous; and even now the names of Adam Smith, Sir William Hamilton, Lockhart, and the present Lord Justice General of Scotland, are not unworthy to stand beside those of the most distinguished among former scholars. Yet I think the Exhibitioners who came after Shairp owed a good deal of their friendly reception to the place

which he had secured for them by his personal popularity and his intellectual reputation. Among those who came immediately
after him were his future brother-in-law,
Henry Douglas, Sir Francis Sandford, and
Patrick Cumin, Secretary to the Education
Office. Shairp and all the rest of us felt
both the pleasure, and the enlargement to
our whole nature, of this intimate association with young Englishmen of culture,
promise, and social vivacity ; many of
whom, in their turn, I am sure, felt the
new zest given to the genial enlivenment
and the varied intellectual life of the college by this Scottish leaven introduced
among them.

In his first term his old love of hunting
had a sharp struggle with his love of reading. I remember hearing, partly from himself and partly from some one else, that
in the early days of his residence, before
he had made many acquaintances, feeling
depressed by the novelty of his position,
he determined to cheer himself by a day's
hunting. Some of the older members of
the " fast set " (as it was called) were out
on the same day, and when they came back
to Hall there was a general inquiry as to

who the freshman was who had ridden so well and hard. He was immediately asked by one of them to his rooms, and as they were a manly and cheerful set of men, with whose life in the open air he had a fellow-feeling, if he had been of weaker character, or less confirmed intellectual pursuits, he might have drifted permanently into the set which was first opened to him. But another rumor soon got abroad about him which reached the older reading-men, who had been at first rather shy of him, owing to his fame in the hunting-field, — that there was a freshman in college who possessed a translation of Kant, and was believed to know all about it. I have heard it said, though I cannot vouch for the accuracy of the report, that the book was borrowed by the college tutor, who, a few years later, did much to make the study of philosophy more systematic in Oxford, and that the reading of it was his first initiation into the subject. Shairp soon formed his chief friendships among the scholars and reading-men, and became himself one among the latter.

The life of a reading-man was then somewhat different from what it is now. The range of reading was more limited, and examinations were fewer. There was, in fact, for honor-men, only one examination of any importance — that at the end of his three, or, in some cases, four years — to which he looked forward from the beginning of his time. This long postponement of their trial gave ample scope for idleness in the first and second year, and many largely availed themselves of their opportunities in that way. But to those who read steadily it gave " leisure to grow wise," to assimilate the thought and substance of their books, and to read much of poetry and philosophy besides, for its own sake, which had a no less important bearing on their mental development. The accurate study of the form and language of the books was not, as it is at present, sharply separated from the sympathetic study of their substance and thought. Scholarship was carried on, as I am inclined to think it ought always to be, side by side with literature, philosophy, and history, and not abruptly separated by an intermediate examination. All of them formed part of the work of each year. Shairp's chief difficulty was, I think, with his scholarship, especially (as it was

with all the Scotchmen) with composition,
which was taught very thoroughly in English schools at an age when the imitative
faculty is most flexible, and before the active powers of thought and of the assimila-
tion of knowledge are developed.

Good Latin composition was a *sine quâ
non* for success in every Oxford examination. The late Rector of Lincoln, in one of
the bitter criticisms which he has left on
record of the Oxford of his days, both un-
reformed and reformed, speaks somewhere
of the college tutor of the old school cov-
ering his intellectual nakedness with " his
rag of Latin prose." Shairp, by dint of a
good deal of uncongenial labor, did acquire
this accomplishment, and I think he felt
that he had got good by the discipline,
though in his case it was somewhat against
the grain. He had, however, real pleasure
in getting up his books, especially his poets
(among whom, I think, Æschylus was his
favorite), and the " Ethics " of Aristotle.
His previous reading made the philosophy
— or " science," as it used to be called, *a
non lucendo* — interesting and familiar to
him. The range of ethical study was not
large. It comprised the " Rhetoric " and

" Ethics " of Aristotle, Butler's " Sermons,"
and the moral consciousness and experience
of the individual student himself and of his
private " coach." Yet this teaching, narrow as it looks, really called out the faculty
and habit of ethical insight and criticism ;
and many men who were educated under it
would in after life acknowledge that it was
the most powerful influence in their intellectual development. Readers of his life
will remember how highly the use of the
" Ethics," as a text-book, was valued by Dr.
Arnold. The range of history, too, was limited to Herodotus, Thucydides, the first decade of Livy, and occasionally the Annals
or Histories of Tacitus. The works neither
of Grote nor Mommsen had then appeared.
The student had to work out historical
problems a good deal for himself. Yet that
the study of Herodotus and Thucydides,
read and re-read by the light of Thirlwall
and Arnold, and of Livy by the light of
Niebuhr, was a good historical " propædeu-
tic " may be learned from the testimony of
an historian who was trained by it, and
whose time at Oxford was coincident with
Shairp's, — Professor Freeman.

But there were other more powerful intellectual forces acting on susceptible minds, then, than that of the regular studies of the place. By far the most searching and moving of these was that of Dr. Newman, then at the very zenith of his influence. No better account has ever been given of that influence, no juster tribute has ever been paid to the genius, sincerity, and by magical spell of him who wielded it, than that given by Shairp in his essay on Keble. He never was in the least inclined to give assent to Dr. Newman's logical position, or to accept his theological doctrines; and he had a positive repugnance to the form which these doctrines assumed in some of his adherents. But he had the sincerest admiration of the high, pure, unworldly type of character realized by him, and by some of the older among his followers and of those closest to him in personal sympathy. The whole attitude of Dr. Newman, then and afterwards, touched his imagination; and I remember long afterwards his characterizing him, in two lines of his friend Matthew Arnold, as

> "One of that small transfigured band
> Whom the world could not tame."

It was also during Shairp's time at Oxford

that the influence of Dr. Arnold, beyond his own immediate sphere, began to be felt. This was partly a continuation of his Rugby influence, transmitted through his pupils, some of the best of whom were, and continued through all his life to be, among Shairp's most intimate friends. But it had been brought more immediately to bear on Oxford by his recent appointment to the Professorship of Modern History, and the delivery of a course of lectures, probably the most eloquent, in the best sense of the word, ever listened to by an Oxford audience; and the startling suddenness of his death, though it entailed a great loss to English education, and a still greater and permanent loss to English literature, added to the impression produced by his teaching and personality; and this was still further deepened by the publication of his Life a year or two later. Though Shairp did not sympathize with Dr. Arnold's political position either in church or state, yet I have often heard him express the strongest personal and literary admiration for him; and he, as well as Dr. Newman, is to be included among those who helped to form his intellectual and religious life.

But a larger wave of imaginative and emotional influence, which had begun elsewhere and soon afterwards spread over the whole nation, then reached Oxford, and Shairp was one of the first to feel it, — the influence of Carlyle. I remember his telling me how it reached him.

He had been tired by his morning's reading, depressed by the weather, which was too bad even for an Oxford "constitutional," and had gone, in a state of intellectual depression, into a bookseller's shop, had seen and immediately bought the four or five volumes of "Miscellanies," which had just appeared, and carried them back to his rooms. The first essay on which he came was that on "Edward Irving," which he read and re-read, walking about his room, feeling himself, as he said, possessed and carried away by a new passion, unlike to what he had ever experienced before. I can yet recall how he repeated with deep feeling, and that fine musical intonation which he gave to anything in verse or prose (as, for example, passages in Newman's "Sermons") which deeply moved him, such sentences as "His was the truest, bravest, brotherliest human

heart mine ever came in contact with,"
etc. ; and that, " He sleeps with his fathers
in that loved birth-land. Mighty Babylon
rages on by him henceforth unheeded forever."

This admiration, mingled with a kind of
affectionate regard (though I don't remember that he had any personal acquaintance
with him), continued through his life. But
he had little sympathy with his later attitude to the world, and not much with some
of the later developments of his literary
style. All satire, even the greatest and
most searching, was uncongenial to him ;
and that will partly explain his imperfect
appreciation of one of the most powerful manifestations of Burns's many-sided
genius.

It was about this time, too, that the two
volumes which first established Tennyson's
right to rank among great English poets
appeared. Shairp acknowledged the rising
star, but this did not make him, as it did
some of his younger associates, falter in his
devotion to the older light, which was still
shining. His taste in poetry had been
early formed, and he was slow to admit
even the two greatest among our living

poets to an equal place in his heart with
the older objects of his love. His love of
poetry was rather deep and vivid than
many-sided. He was inclined to set his
face against any new heresy of criticism, —
any

"Vana superstitio, veterumque ignara deorum,"

to which young Oxford then, as I fancy it
still is, was prone. The worst of those
heresies, which some adopted who should
have known better, and which they probably outlived, was one which, if it had not
its origin, at least found its strongest support, in Carlyle, — a tendency to disparage
Scott, not only as a poet but as a great cre-
ative genius. Against this heresy Shairp
always indignantly protested, and I can remember the warmth with which he replied
to some shallow but perhaps not altogether
untrue criticism on some of his weaker
places : "I would as soon think of criticis-
ing my own father as Sir Walter."

The first time I saw him was in the October term of 1842, the beginning of his third
year of residence, when I was in Oxford for
a few days as candidate for a scholarship.
I had heard much of him in Glasgow, where
he left behind him a great personal and

intellectual reputation. On arriving in Oxford I heard still more of him from the Snell Exhibitioners, who immediately preceded me, and whom I had known in Glasgow. He had in the previous June added distinction to their body and to his college by gaining the Newdigate prize for an English poem on the subject of Charles XII., which was justly regarded as the poem of most original power which had appeared since Stanley's "Gipsies." I have heard that it received some mark of recognition, in the way of letter or some other token, from old Bernadotte, who was then king of Sweden. It is one among very few prize poems, indeed, that one can still read with pleasure and admiration. To those who knew him it has the interest of giving his own fresh impressions of Nature derived from those wanderings in spring, among

" The dark woods and the silent hills "

of his country, which had already begun. I can recall the room in which I first saw him, and his appearance as he stood on the hearth-rug in front of the fire. He was a little older than most undergraduates are, and he looked perhaps a little older than he was, — I mean more manly-looking and more fully developed. He received me, as a new-comer from Scotland and Glasgow, with that frank, kindly greeting — "the smile in the eye as well as on the lip," as in the young shepherd in " Theocritus " — which was never absent in our meetings after longer or shorter separation in later years. I retain the impression rather of the high spirit and animation, and of a kind of generous pride characteristic of him, than of the milder, far-away, contemplative look which became familiar to one in later years. Except that he became bald and somewhat gray, he never seemed to change much in other ways during all the subsequent years that I knew him; and if he looked a little older than he was in youth, he retained much of fresh youthfulness in his appearance when he was nearly an old man. I remember being present (then for the first time) at the annual dinner in which the Scotchmen of the University celebrate, or used to celebrate, St. Andrew's Day, and that Shairp was the life and soul of it, as he was on all similar occasions, speaking with that happy mixture of serious enthusiasm, and playful or bantering allusion, which best befits convivial oratory.

When I came up as a freshman a few
months later he asked me to his rooms, and
I felt pride and pleasure, in the beginning
of my career at Oxford, in any kindly no-
tice or encouragement from one who was
himself so much of a *vir laudatus.* But I
did not become really intimate with him till
the Christmas vacation of 1845, when, for
about a fortnight, he, Walrond, and I were
the sole occupants of the college ; he reading for a fellowship, Walrond and I for our
degrees. He had taken his degree, I think,
in the Easter term of 1844, and like a large
proportion of the men about that time of
most original gifts, and who have since
gained the greatest distinction in literature, — including Clough, M. Arnold, Mr.
Froude, Mr. Freeman, M. Pattison, Sir A.
Grant, and others, — he was placed in the
second class. We dined together daily, and
sat for two or three hours in one another's
rooms in the evening ; and as Walrond
generally preferred tennis to a " constitutional " in the afternoons, I was sometimes
his only companion, as often afterwards, in
the familiar round of walks in the country
about Oxford. I can remember the pleasure and the profit with which I used then

to hear him discuss speculative questions with serious and animated interest, or chant old ballads, and poems of Wordsworth, then unknown to me. I don't remember that he ever expressed much pleasure in the scenes through which our walks lay. The country about Oxford, as everywhere else, looks very different in January from what it looks in June, and the daily routine of constitutionalizing is apt to deaden the sense of beauty. But that both his eye and heart did take in the characteristic charm of the place and its surrounding scenery, one could tell afterwards from the way in which he used to speak of the truth, both real and ideal, with which M. Arnold has, in " The Scholar-Gipsy " and " Thyrsis," made that charm live for all time in English literature. Yet his love of nature, deep and passionate as it was, was in him intertwined with his affections. In later years he came to love Oxford next after Scotland, from the memory of happy study and happier friendships formed there. And when he went back to it in those years, I think there were few among the habitual residents in the colleges more sensible of its beauty.

The only fellowship practically open to

him then was the Oriel, for which, although
sound scholarship was a requisite, the more
special refinements of scholarship (such as
Greek verse, etc.), which were necessary for
the Balliol, — the only other competition at
that time open to Scotchmen, — were not
demanded. General intellectual promise
and originality were looked for rather than
either large or exact knowledge. Intellectual originality is a much better and more
attractive thing than acquired knowledge or
scholarship, if it could be only ascertained
by as definite tests. Where there are two
or three different kinds of original talent in
the field, it becomes a matter of individual
taste which should be preferred, and it is
hardly possible that fortune should not
have some share in deciding the issue.
Shairp was unsuccessful in the competition ; but it was known that some among
the examiners, not the least qualified to estimate mental power, formed a very favor-
able opinion of his work.

It became necessary for him to decide on
a profession. He never had any inclina-
tion, and probably not much aptitude, for
the bar. In many ways he would have
made an admirable clergyman, and what he

has written in his essay on Keble shows
what attraction the beauty as well as the
goodness which could be realized in the
life of a country vicar had for him. But
the English Church was not that in which
he had been brought up; and with neither
of the phases of opinion by which the men
of most intellect and culture were then
characterized — the new development of
High Church doctrine, and the more advanced theology of the Broad Church —
was he in perfect accord.

He went, I think, a certain length with
the adherents of the Broad Church, and
among his intimate friends were the men
of most vivid imagination and of the greatest speculative originality belonging to that
school. Some of his other friends, with
whom he may have talked more unreserv-
edly on this subject than he was inclined to
do with me, will probably say something
about the grounds of his religious convictions, which continued henceforth very firm,
and became the chief regulative power in
his life. His nature was eminently conservative both in politics and religion, and
his conservatism was based on feeling
rather than on argument. He had more

trust in what he had seen work for good on
personal character, than he had expectation
of good from novelties of opinion. Religion had never been presented to him in
his childhood in a way to cloud his happiness, and it was associated with all that was
dear to him in his home life. I think it
was to that simple belief, from which he
had never gone far, that he returned. So
far as he was influenced by doctrinal discussion, it was not to the writings of any English divines, but to the works of Dr. M'Leod
Campbell, and of his friend Mr. Erskine of
Linlathen, that he seemed to feel his in-
debtedness. So far as my own relations
with him were concerned, his religious convictions and his religious life seemed only
to add greater seriousness, consistency, and
hopefulness to a character in all its human
aspects noble and beautiful.

His difficulties as to a profession were
settled by his receiving an invitation from
Dr. Tait — then head-master of Rugby, who
had been senior tutor of Balliol when Shairp
entered, and as having himself been a Snell
Exhibitioner, and probably also a family
friend, had from the first taken a great interest in him — to accept a mastership in

the school. Of his work in the school, and
of his personal influence on his pupils, you
will no doubt hear from some of his surviving colleagues, and from some younger men
who received from him their first literary
and intellectual impulse. I saw a good deal
of him in those days, and was often at
Rugby, — once for several weeks at a time,
— sometimes as his guest and sometimes as
the guest of his friend and colleague, Walrond. The routine of work, while making
him less desultory, did not seem to me to
quench to any degree the ardor of his enthusiasm either for poetry or speculative
discussion. He was then, as he always continued to be, an animated and excellent
talker, and I can remember some of his en-
counters with one who only the other day
was still a vigorous veteran of controversy,
Mr. Bonamy Price, — one in particular, at
the house of the latter, on some point of
doctrinal theology, which almost assumed
the proportions of an old disputation.
Shairp took the first innings, and a long
and admirable innings he played. The
match, however, was drawn; for Shairp
and one or two of those present had fallen
asleep long before his keen and clear-

headed opponent had made up his score.
He had great pleasure in his intercourse
with his more advanced pupils; but he
probably grew a little weary of the drudg-
ery of teaching boys in one of the lower
forms. He got fully to appreciate the good
of the English public-school system, — the
friendships which were formed by it; the
manliness of character, the spirit of honor,
and the frankness of manner conspicuous
in the better type of public-school men. He
thought, however, that it had a tendency to
dwarf originality. It is true that a public school prepares men to live in and act
upon the world, rather than to live apart
from it and to act upon it from a distance,
as Wordsworth or Carlyle did. . . . But
Shairp would have admitted, I think, that
for one genius lost by the training of a public school, a hundred clever lads were im-
proved by having the conceit or eccentricity
thereby knocked out of them. It was his
appreciation of its good influence on character and manners that made him anxious to
realize, and for a time successful in realizing, something of the same influence in the
College Hall of St. Andrews.

Though he found in his Rugby life a

sphere of usefulness, and had much enjoyment in his intercourse with his colleagues
and his older and abler pupils, yet he
longed for more freedom to develop the
speculative and poetical faculty within him.
I had heard him say long before that he
would rather use his practical power of
work in Scotland than anywhere else.
When, accordingly, in the year 1857, Dr.
Pyper, the Professor of Latin in St. Andrews, was permanently disabled by bad
health, Shairp, though at a great pecuniary
sacrifice, applied for and accepted the position of his assistant. The position which
had held out most attraction to him when
he was at Oxford was that of a Scotch professor ; but he thought then more of a Chair
of Moral Philosophy, for which he was admirably qualified, had he been appointed to
one while the speculative impulse was still
strong upon him, than of one of the classical chairs.

He had a genuine appreciation for the
great Greek and Roman writers, and he
held that there was as yet at least no other
equally humanizing discipline for those who
were able and willing to profit by it. Still
the classics were, as he said, not " his first

loves ; " and I have heard him humorously
complain of the weariness of the daily
round of " vocables," — a word much in the
mouth of one of our colleagues in looking
over the papers in the Bursary Competition, at which lively occupation, which he
keenly enjoyed himself, he used to keep
us out of bed, though hardly awake, till
four in the morning. But he recognized
and availed himself of the greater scope af-
forded in a professorial class for vitalizing
the reading of the classics, developing the
literary interest of the subject, and for that
unsystematic ethical teaching — the teaching of " humanity " — involved in it. The
work of teaching the language in a sound,
scholar-like way, I need hardly say, he performed faithfully. I think the professors
in the Arts Faculties of the Scottish universities would feel along with me how
much the pleasure and usefulness of their
work depends on their colleagues in the
subject cognate to their own ; how it takes
half the heart out of their work if their
yoke-fellow pulls the other way, teaches
what they feel called on to unteach, and
unteaches what they feel called on to teach ;
or if he is one between whom and himself

there exists no personal or intellectual sympathy.

I had gone to St. Andrews three or four years before Shairp came there, as assistant to the Professor of Greek, who was incapacitated for work for several years before his death. Shairp and I worked together for six or seven years, first as assistants, doing all the work of the professor, and afterwards as professors, he of Latin and I of Greek. It would have been impossible to have had a colleague more loyal and sympathetic, one with whom one could work in more perfect harmony and mutual confidence, — an advantage which, if I may be allowed to say so here, I again enjoy in the fullest possible measure. None of his colleagues took a warmer personal interest in the students than Shairp, especially in some of the poorer among them, and those who had enjoyed fewest previous advantages in whom he recognized some finer traits of character. From his sense of responsibility and from the influence of his English experience, he wished to exercise a more direct moral influence among them than was in accordance with the traditions of student life in the Scotch universities; and this had a tendency to rouse in some of the rougher set the *nemo me impune lacessit* sentiment, which is perhaps stronger in the Scotch student than in any other members of the community. With the same view, he coöperated most cordially with Principal Forbes in the establishment of the College Hall, which for two or three years, under the first Warden, — who had the happy tact of hitting the right mean between freedom and restraint, and of being himself both the companion and the guardian of those under his charge, — promised to be a most successful experiment, an experiment which, for some reason or other, failed to maintain itself; and which, though often talked of, has never been renewed in any of our universities. Perhaps the much-dreaded danger of the "Anglification" of our indigenous customs and manners is an obstacle to the introduction of such alien institutions.

We were most fortunate in our colleagues, and in the social circle which their families and other families in the town then formed. There was first the veteran Scottish representative of science, Sir David Brewster, who to us new-comers, though we were quite unfit to enter into his special pursuits, was always the most simple and delightful of associates. When he removed to Edinburgh his place was filled by another representative of science, equally illustrious, Principal Forbes. Between him and Shairp there was for a time some friction, arising chiefly out of difference of opinion about college matters. They were both men of a pure and disinterested type of character, but they were essentially different in temperament. Shairp was, beyond almost all other men, warm and open; Forbes was outwardly cold and reserved, perhaps even suspicious, till he knew well those with whom he was dealing. Gradually, however, as they worked together in college business, Shairp came to recognize the single-minded devotion to duty and the warmth and sensitiveness of feeling which lay under that outward reserve; and, with the generosity native to him, he grew into an appreciative admiration and trust, all the warmer and firmer because he had at first misjudged him. Tulloch was Principal of St. Mary's, still a young man, in the vigorous prime of his intellectual force and genial companionship. Not to speak of some others among the professors, with

whom Shairp was always in friendly relations, we had for one year among us the eminent Cambridge mathematician and discov-
erer, Professor Adams. The Logic Chair
was filled at first by Professor Spalding, an
earnest and successful teacher of his subject, and a man of fine literary accomplishment; but his bad health, though it did
not prevent his doing his work faithfully
till the last, preventing our seeing much of
him socially. He was succeeded in 1860
by Veitch, now Professor of Logic in Glasgow, and he soon became one of Shairp's
most valued and sympathetic friends. The
intellectual bond of sympathy between them
was partly, I suppose, speculative agree-
ment, though Shairp's speculative interest
was directed mainly to ethics, and to some
ultimate problems of metaphysics connected
with theology, and not much to the province
of logic and psychology; but the chief and
most lasting bond was a common love of
ballad-poetry and the Border country, both
of which were probably better known to
them than to any other men of their time.

But the centre of all the intellectual and
social life of the University and of the town
was Professor Ferrier. He inspired in the

students a feeling of affectionate devotion as well as admiration, such as I have hardly ever known inspired by any teacher; and to many of them his mere presence and bearing in the class-room was a large element in a liberal education. By all his colleagues he was esteemed as a man of most sterling honor, a stanch friend, and a most humorous and delightful companion. Shairp, though he had no pretension to original humor, had a great enjoyment in it, and in all lively and harmless fun; and there certainly never was a household known to either of us in which the spirit of racy and original humor and fun was so exuberant and spontaneous, in every member of it, as that of which the Professor and his wife — the most gifted and brilliant, and most like her father, of the three gifted daughters of Christopher North — were the heads. Our evenings there generally ended in the Professor's study, where he was always ready to discuss, either from a serious or humorous point of view, with him or any one else (not without congenial accompaniments), the various points of his metaphysical system till the morning was well advanced. Grant, too, was much there in

those days, taking his part in the philosophical, literary, and humorous talk of his
future father-in-law, and bringing to us re-
ports of the latest developments in the ever-
shifting phases of Oxford taste, opinion, and
educational machinery.

One source of pleasure in the life Shairp
felt, I think, more than any of us, — the
delight in the place itself, in its picturesque
shores and ruins, and its historic memories. During his summers he continued
his wanderings over the more familiar and
some of the wildest parts of the Highlands,
and it was chiefly in these wanderings that
he had gradually shaped the poems, expressive of the characteristic sentiment, both
as regards outward nature and the spirit of
the people, of Highlands, Lowlands, and
Borders, which were given to the world in
1863 in the volume called, from the principal poem, " Kilmahoe."

From the time I left St. Andrews in
1863, though we saw much less of one another, there was no abatement of our friendship. . . . His talk was always delightful,
and was always about the things and subjects which really interested him. We met
him once or twice in Oxford on our visits to

the master of Balliol, during the summer
terms, when he used to give his lectures as
Professor of Poetry. He had great pleasure in his life there, in the beauty of the
place, in the revival of old and the making
of new friendships among the younger men.
Once, on their way back to their summer
home in Perthshire, he and Mrs. Shairp
passed a few days with us here in the Glen-
kens of Galloway. This was one of the
few among the picturesque parts of Scotland which had hitherto remained unknown
to him. I have never seen any one enjoy
this country more. His historic feeling was
touched by a visit to Kenmure Castle, by
the sight of the pictures of the men and
women of "Kenmure's line," who played a
bold part in the first Jacobite rising, and
also by seeing the desolate hills and moors
around Carsphairn, among which there still
linger memories of the Covenanters. With
these two antagonistic causes he had an
impartial sympathy. Like Scott, he was
attracted by what was chivalrously daring
or grimly earnest in our national history,
to the disregard of what was politic and
economic. He was present at our Tercen-
tenary Celebration in the spring of 1884,

when, on the proposal of his friend, Sir
Alexander Grant, he, among many distinguished men from all countries, received
the degree of LL. D.

The last time I saw him was in Decem-
ber of that year, when he and I walked together in the sad and solemn procession at
the funeral of our old Balliol and Oriel
friend. The thought occurred to both of
us, as we talked over the past, how strange
it would have seemed to us if, some forty
years before, when we were all three young
men together, with an uncertain future before us, we had had, while all the interven-
ing years remained unknown to us, a pro-
phetic vision of that spectacle of which we
formed a part, and some intimation of its
meaning. He came back with me to my
house, and I remember, as I was somewhat
ill at the time, how kindly and earnestly he
urged me to get leave of absence till after
Christmas, offering to come and do my
work for me himself. I mention this because it was one among several occasions in
my life in which I had proof not only of his
kindest sympathy, but of his most active
friendliness. On one important occasion I
now know that he acted towards me with a

magnanimous disregard of his own interest,
of which very few men indeed are capable.
Though I could not specify these services
without entering on details which concern
myself alone, there are none ever rendered
to me by any one for which I feel a more
lasting gratitude. . . . My last association
with him was of walking, along with old
college friends of his and mine, and friends
and former colleagues from St. Andrews, in
the garden and the fields about his home
in Linlithgowshire, on the morning of the
bright autumn day on which he was borne
to the family burial-place. It seemed then
that there could have been no more pious
and beautiful close to a pious and beautiful
life, — none more fit to leave on the mind,
in the words of a poem which was a great
favorite of his, " happy thoughts about the
dead." . . . He realized his poetry in his
life.

The biographies of men of genius show
that sometimes, along with high aspiration
and heroic effort, there coexists a " seamy
side " in their lives, and that the fame they
enjoy is counterbalanced by something un-
happy in their lot. Those most intimate
with him never saw any " seamy side " in

Shairp's life ; and his lot was eminently a
happy one. He had not, and he never desired, great worldly success. He may have
had at times, more than many of his friends
and social equals, to feel the strain of the
res angusta domi. But it came naturally
to him to realize the precept of his first
teacher, and to combine " plain living with
high thinking." I remember when the St.
Andrews revenues were, owing to the agri-
cultural depression, at their lowest, his saying with a kind of gallant pride, " It is
nonsense making a poor mouth about these
things." He received from Nature a com-
bination of the courage and independent
spirit of a man, with the refinement and
ready sympathy of a woman. And this
natural endowment was tempered into a
consistent character by constant watchful-
ness against any assertion of self, in the way
either of indulgence, or interest, or vanity.
He was eminently happy in his early home-
life, and in the home of his later life ; and
the happiness of his later home did not
weaken his tie to the older one. He was
also most happy in the number and quality
of his friends, and while he went on till the
end of his life adding to their number, he

never, I am sure, lost one through any fault
or neglect of his own. He was by no means
too facile in forming friendships, but when
once he trusted a man it would have been
no light cause that afterwards alienated
him.

He was, I think, a true discerner of character, and what he looked for in any one he
cared for was that he should be genuine, —
his real self. He regarded with good-hu-
mored amusement all affectation and pre-
tense, and all ambition in a man to appear
or to be greater or more distinguished than
nature and circumstances fitted him to be.
For anything false and base in the relations
of men to one another he felt an indignant
scorn ; and he would have been more chari-
table in judging of it if the wrong were
done to himself than if it were done to a
friend or even a stranger. As he had a
quick sense of personal dignity, and a generous impetuosity of spirit, it was possible
that he might sometimes take, and sometimes, though rarely, give offense ; but if
this happened, he was always prompt to
receive or to make acknowledgment ; and
the matter was never afterwards remembered. At no time of his life would any

one have said in his presence anything
essentially coarse or irreverent; or if he had
done so once, he would not have repeated the
experiment. But not to speak of the specially Christian graces which adorned him,
there were in his human relations two qualities prized equally by Christian and Pa-
gan, especially conspicuous, — candor and
generosity. Dr. Newman, in the "Gram-
mar of Assent," speaks of the way in which,
in our youth, we read some of the classical
writers, and think we understand them, and
he shows how different that understanding
is from the truer insight we gain into their
meaning when we have had experience of
life. It seems to me, in thinking of Shairp,
that I only now understand the full human
feeling and human experience compressed
into the "sad earnestness and vivid exactness" of lines often read and often quoted
with perhaps an incomplete realization of
their meaning, —

> "Incorrupta fides nudaque veritas
> Quando ullum inveniet parem?"

THOMAS ERSKINE.

[IN THE FORM OF A LETTER ADDRESSED TO REV. DR. HANNA, EDITOR OF "LETTERS OF THOMAS ERSKINE OF LINLATHEN."]

You have often urged me to attempt some connected narrative of the life and character of our revered friend, the late Mr. Erskine of Linlathen, and I have often myself felt a strong desire to do so; but as soon as the desire has arisen, I have been restrained by a sense of utter inability. I felt the truth of those words which Dr. Macleod Campbell wrote to Bishop Ewing soon after Mr. Erskine's death: "No man is able to say to those who knew him not what he was; no man could say this to those who knew him in a way that they would feel satisfying." All that I shall now attempt is to put together such recollections of him as I can give, in the hope that these may be found in keeping with the impression made by those delightful letters which you are publishing.

Although it was as a spiritual teacher

working by voice and pen that Mr. Erskine
was known to the world, yet one cannot
fully understand his mind and influence
without taking some account of his human
temperament and earthly circumstances.
In him, hardly less than in more mundane
characters, the race from which he came
and the people who surrounded his childhood had much to do with making him
what he ultimately became. He himself
would have been one of the last to under-
rate what he owed to his ancestry. On
either side he was sprung from a far-de-
scended and gracious race, and among
these his kindred he passed a childhood
and youth sheltered from those early shocks
and jars which probably lie at the root of
much of the unkindness and asperity there
is in the world. Equally on his father's
and mother's side he came from what the
late biographer of Walter Scott used to call,
with so much satisfaction, " a fine old Scottish family." Often of a winter evening, as
with one or two guests Mr. Erskine drew
in his chair round the dining-room fire at
Linlathen, he would look up at the family
pictures that hung round the room, and tell
their history, and remark on their charac-

ters. When he looked at the portrait of
" the Black Colonel," as he was called,
partly from his swarthy complexion, perhaps, too, from the dark armor in which he
is encased, he would speak of him with a
peculiar twinkle in his eye and a humorous
smile on his face. Among the virtues you
have attributed to the Black Colonel, that
bulwark of Presbyterianism, there is one
you have omitted, — his great love of litiga-
tion. His great-grandson, however, used to
tell how, on his death-bed, he is reported
to have said, " Haena I thretty gude ga'in
pleas on hand, and that fule Jock will hae
compounded them a' a fortnicht after I 'm
dead." That " fule Jock " was his son, the
great Scottish jurist, author of the " Insti-
tutes." His picture hangs near his father's,
and his pale, chiseled, refined features form
a striking contrast to the broad, swarthy,
pugnative visage of the Black Colonel.
Mr. Erskine would also dwell lovingly on
an excellent copy by Urquhart of Raeburn's
beautiful picture of a refined old lady's face.
This was the portrait of the Hon. Christian
Mackay, daughter of the third Lord Reay,
which hung beside that of her grave, earnest husband, Dr. John Erskine, minister of

Greyfriars, who was Mr. Erskine's uncle. In the late Raeburn Exhibition in Edinburgh, the original of this picture of Christian Mackay was regarded as one of the finest of the many fine old-lady portraits by that great artist. He would also speak of the strong, homely sense, mingled with genial yet refined humanity, that looked out from the face of Lady Christian Bruce, the wife of his uncle James, the laird of Cardross. Most of the pictures that hung round that dining-room belonged to his father's side of the house.

Of his maternal ancestors, though there was but one picture on the wall, the images dwelt no less vividly in his heart. At Airth Castle, his mother's home, the happiest days of his childhood were spent. The old lady of Airth, his maternal grandmother, you have yourself well described, reading her English-Church service every Sunday to her family in her own drawing-room, while the Presbyterian worship was going on in the kirk, which then stood hard by the castle. The old place of Airth is one deeply to impress itself on a young imagination.

Out of the carse of Falkirk, that great

dead-level plain that stretches from Falkirk
to Stirling, which, as the great battlefield
of Scotland, holds in Scottish history, as
Dean Stanley has suggested, the same place
which the plain of Esdraelon held in the
history of Israel, — out of that carse, about
a mile inland from the Links of Forth, rises
a scarpment or ridge of sandstone abruptly
breaking from the surrounding flats.   On
the edge of that scarpment stands the old
castle, originally a square peel tower with
pent-house roof, like those common all over
Scotland.   To that tower has been built,
on a long, high line of building, with crow-
stepped gables, a steep roof, and dormer
windows projecting from it.   This range of
building forms the later dwelling-house, all
that was there in Mr. Erskine's childhood ;
though since then there have been made
quite modern and not very congruous addi-
tions.   This long building, flanked on the
west by the older tower, looks down, over a
small precipice, on a quaint garden beneath,
and beyond the garden are old trees and a
lazy stream lingering towards the Forth.
The house fronts southward, and across the
dead-level carse the windows look far away
to the rising ground of Falkirk muir, the

scene of two great battles. Contiguous to
the house, on the northeast side, is the old
churchyard, full of ancient graves and gray
tombstones. A church must once have
stood there, but it has disappeared. Behind the house, to north and west, long
straight avenues and park trees stretch on
towards the grounds of Dunmore Park. It
is almost an ideal abode of an ancient Scottish family, like those Walter Scott loved
to picture. Such, outwardly, was the place
and neighborhood where Thomas Erskine
drank in his first impressions of a world in
which he was to abide for fourscore years.
For the associations of a mere town house
in childhood go for little compared with
those of the first country home.

The inside of Airth Castle was warm to
him with much loving-kindness and old-
fashioned yet refined simplicity. The old
servant, himself quite a part of the family,
who spent his whole life-time at Airth, lives
in Dean Ramsay's well-known story about
Mrs. Moray of Abercairney and the salt-
spoon, a story, by the way, with which Mr.
Erskine furnished the dean. But to that
quaint example of

"The constant service of the antique world,"

Dean Ramsay has not added one pathetic incident with which Mr. Erskine used to accompany it. That old family man-servant, John Campbell, lived to see Mrs. Graham's eldest son, the heir of the house, go to India in his country's service. Years after, the ship which was expected to bring him back to England brought the news of his death. On the day when the new mourning suit which John was to wear for his young master's death was laid down on the table before him, he fainted away. That kind of faithful affection in a domestic servant, common enough at the beginning of this century, has become rarer nowadays.

Airth, Kippenross, Keir, Ochtertyre, Cardross, with occasional visits to Ardoch, his grandmother's home, and to Abercairney, — the summers of childhood and boyhood spent in these melted into him with associations of beauty and ancestral repose which were indelible, and the warm atmosphere of human life that then surrounded him sweetened his whole nature to the core. It had no doubt much to do with drawing out that deep and tender affectionateness which made him, all life through, the much-loving and much-beloved man he was.

In this he was very unlike most men.
Hearts, more or less, I suppose, most of us
have, but we keep them so close-cased and
padlocked, we wear an outside so hard or
dry, that little or none of the love that may
be within escapes to gladden those around
us. And so life passes without any of the
sweetening to society that comes when affection is not only felt but expressed, for to
be of any use to others it must be expressed
in some way. Mr. Erskine was in this
happy above most men, that, being gifted
with a heart more than usually tender and
sympathetic, he had brought with him from
childhood the art of expressing it simply
and naturally. So it was that the loving-
kindness that was in him streamed freely
forth, making the happy happier, and light-
ening the load of the sorrowful. It was as
if inside his man's understanding he hid, as
it were, a woman's heart. And though this
is a thing no early training could have im-
planted, yet, when it was there, the warm
affection that surrounded his boyhood was
the very atmosphere to cherish and expand it.

If this had been all, it might have led to
softness, but the society of his childhood,

though based on affection, had enough of
the old Scottish nerve and intellect in it to
keep it from degenerating into sentimental-
ism.   His own busy intellect, too, was early
stirring, and the winter home of his mother
in St. David Street was pervaded by that
old-world simplicity and frugality which is
so bracing to character. Besides, even if
the boy's early years had been too tenderly
nurtured, school life, as it then existed, especially in the rough old High School of Edinburgh, was sure to give scope enough for
the hardy virtues.

Although I had long known Mr. Erskine
by reputation and through mutual friends,
it was not until the year 1854 that I became
personally acquainted with him. As I happened to be in Scotland in the winter of
that year, his cousin, Miss Jane Stirling,
wrote to him that I was anxious to meet
him, and he at once invited me to visit him
at Linlathen.

It was, I think, on a Saturday afternoon,
the 7th of January, in that year, that he
received me in that library at Linlathen
which his friends so well remember.   I
had not been any time with him before
he opened on those subjects which lay al-

ways deepest in his thoughts. Often during that visit, in the library, or in walks
after dark up and down the corridor, or,
when the weather allowed, in walks about
the grounds, those subjects were renewed.
The one thing that first struck me at that
time was his entire openness of mind ; his
readiness to hear whatever could be urged
against his own deepest convictions; the
willingness with which he welcomed any
difficulties felt by others, and the candor
with which he answered them from his
own experience and storehouse of reflec-
tion. He exemplified that text which he
often quoted, " The heart of the righteous
man studieth to answer." This was a characteristic of him which is not often found
in men so religious. Commonly the state-
ment of any view, very unlike that which
they have been accustomed to hold, shocks
them ; and younger inquirers, seeing that
they are thought impious or give pain,
cease to reveal their thoughts, and intercourse is at an end. With Mr. Erskine it
was just the reverse of this. His whole
manner and spirit elicited confidence from
younger men. No thought could ever have
occurred to them which, if they were serious

about it, they need have hesitated to tell
him.   And it would seldom be that they
did not find in his replies something really
helpful, or at least something well worth
their pondering.

The following are some notes of his conversations made during that first visit: —

What is the true guide ?

Answer : I fall back more and more on
first principles.   The conscience in each
man is the Christ in each man.   It is the
ray of light coming straight from the great
Fountain of light; or rather, it is the eye
guided by the Sun ; or it is the child's shell
murmuring of its native ocean ; or the cord
let down by God into each man by which
He leads each.   Often the string lies quite
slack ; the man is not conscious of the guid-
ance and the guide.   Then the string becomes tight, and the man feels the drawing; he is conscious of God.   The great
thing is to identify duty and conscience
hourly with God.

The universal diffusion of conscience
through all men is Christ in all men, —
" Christ in you the hope of glory."

He was in the man, and the man was
made by Him, and the man knew Him not.

This is true of every man by nature. And the great thing is to become conscious of Him, and to know Him through himself revealed in conscience. "The Spirit (not of the wind) bloweth whither it will, and ye hear the sound thereof, but cannot tell whence it cometh or whither it goeth." But for not being able to tell we are in fault. This is our sin. [This was with Mr. Erskine one favorite gloss upon that text in St. John's Gospel, though I never felt sure that it was a correct one. Besides this, he gave to it other applications.]

"No man hath ascended up to heaven." ... And so it is only Christ in the man, the man who has become one with Christ and Christ-like, in whom the old self is subdued, that can ascend up to heaven.

This light, this conscience, manifests itself often to man as witnessing against his present state, making him feel the hollowness and discomfort of life apart from God. Still, the witnessing against him, — this is Christ within the man grieving for his alienation, calling him to be reconciled. This condemnation and uneasiness of soul is the sound or tone which God's voice takes when speaking in the natural heart. It is

God and Christ calling him to return. This voice of God sounds loud in great crises. If a man were tempted to commit murder, then it would sound more loudly than usual. But it does not then for the first time begin to sound. It has been sounding always, through all his ordinary life, in a low habitual tone, but he has not heard nor cared to hear it.

There is into each man a continual inflowing of the Logos. It is by virtue of Christ being in all men that conscience is universal in men.

" He that answereth before he heareth is a son that causeth shame." So we ought to hear this voice of the Spirit before we act or speak ; we ought to wait for it, and not make haste. " The heart of the righteous studieth to answer." Man ought to wait on this voice, for it is always there, if we would hear it. When our Lord said, " He that hath ears to hear, let him hear," it was this inward ear he meant.

This conscience, this inward light, is the great organ of theology. Only that which commends itself to his conscience, that which each man can feel to be right and true, that only he really believes. What-

ever more he fancies he believes, on authority or otherwise, is not real belief or faith.
But does not this make the old Sophists'
saying true, ἄνθρωπος μέτρον πάντων, or each
man's individual frame or feeling the measure of truth for him? No! For, —

1st. It is of the true nature of conscience not to be individual. Conscience
is not mine, I am conscience's. Each man
does not possess it, but is possessed by it.
It speaks in virtue of a higher light than
itself, of which it declares itself to be but
a ray. It swells outward to Christ, and
finds its fullness only in him and God. It
is their continual witness, referring back
not to itself but to them. Therefore this
light never can cut itself off from its source
and set itself up as an independent authority, for this would be to abdicate its own
nature.

2d. Neither will a man, who is truly
awakened to listen to conscience, set up his
own conscience as a rival of the Bible, and
reject all Scripture that does not at once
commend itself to him. For the conscience
that is true is humble, and feels that it is
but a feeble, struggling ray, and will lie at
the feet of the true light; only it will not

say that it believes anything till it does
believe it, that is, till it feels it to be right
and true. Further than this it cannot go.
That larger light which men may urge on
its acceptance, on the authority of the
church or of Scripture, — it does not deny
this or set itself against it ; only it cannot
take it in, make it its own, till for itself it
sees light through it. It will say, What
you urge me to believe may be true, but I
do not know it to be true now. I may come
to see it, or I may not, but at present I am
not in a condition to witness for it.

Christ is the great universal conscience,
calling to every man, Hear and your soul
shall live, — live to God, die to yourself.

Next day he added this corollary to the
above : God speaks to me in conscience, but
I do not always apprehend his language. I
seek to know and apprehend it, and I find
far more in the Bible than anywhere else
that explains conscience. It may be said,
All things are calls ; all things are intended
to educate men, and so in a sense they are.
But the Bible is so in a peculiar way. I
explain conscience by the Bible, and the
Bible by conscience, both ways ; but still
they meet and illuminate each the other, —
there is no true light, no true conviction.

The gospel history is the consciousness I find within me expressed outwardly. It is only by finding a oneness between the outward history and the inward consciousness that I can understand the history, and the history makes me understand my own consciousness. The history of Jesus Christ, what He sorrowed and suffered, is a perfect outward manifestation of what will go on imperfectly in every man's heart now, just in proportion as he enters into the mind of Christ.

Another day during that visit Mr. Erskine's conversation took this turn: Christ stands to us in two capacities. *First*, as the representative of the Father He came, showing us what is the character of the Father, bringing down to us his holy, righteous, loving purpose towards us. And so He comes down now to each man, is, as it were, again incarnate in each man's conscience, and in that conscience — the true light, the Spirit within each man — He grieves over each man's sin, agonizes for it in each man, "suffers, the just for the unjust;" just as you might conceive the spirit of St. John to enter inside the spirit of Barabbas; St. John's heart to be shut up in

Barabbas's heart, — how it would be pained
and grieved by the dark, polluted environ-
ment in which it found itself! Naturally
it would will itself away from such an
abode. But if it were to stay there, and
though grieving and sore pained yet refuse
to depart till it had purified Barabbas and
won him back to God, in some such way we
may conceive of the Christ indwelling in
each man. Or as an upright, high-minded
elder brother might grieve and feel pain at
seeing some great meanness or base action
in a younger. At first the elder only would
feel pain and grief; the younger would feel
none. But this pain of the elder might, in
time, be seen by the younger, and being
seen might draw him to feel the same, to
enter into the sorrow of the elder, and so
to be of one mind with him, and be delivered from his meanness.

Christ came once, and was manifested
eighteen hundred years ago ; but both before and since that time He has been, as it
were, diffused through humanity, lying at
the bottom of every man as the basis of his
being. It was in Him that God created
man, just as light was the first created
thing, spread abroad diffusedly, but not

gathered up into the sun till the fourth day. So Christ the Head was latent in humanity as the Head, but the Head did not come out and show itself to the senses till the personal Christ appeared in the flesh.

Secondly, Christ's second capacity is as the Head of the whole race. In this capacity He fulfills God's whole will, accepts the suffering which is eternally inseparable from sin, bears it willingly, not indeed to save us from suffering, but to call each of us to accept God's whole will gladly, as He accepted it; to accept suffering when sent, not as a punishment, but as a healing, and so to follow Christ, — to call each to die continually to self, and to accept death as a duty, as the declaration of God's will and purpose towards us; to accept it, not with sullen resignation, or general bare trust in God's mercy, but as feeling that God's purpose for us is always and wholly good, whether in life or death. It is through dying to self continually in life, and at last through actual death willingly borne, only thus that man can overcome. Sin and suffering are eternally connected. The body, which belongs to this seen system of things, to which man alienated from God has sur-

rendered himself, — it is righteous that it
should suffer and die for its sin. And the
spiritual man will see and feel the righteousness of this, and willingly give himself
up to suffering and death. And so Christ
the righteous, as the Elder Brother of our
race, standing at the head of humanity,
willingly entered into and bore this death
which the rest had to bear, and by bearing
He overcame it. And so it is only by clos-
ing with death and suffering willingly (in
the fellowship with Him), by accepting it
as righteous, and apprehending God's righteous, loving purpose in it, that any man can
overcome it. . . .

Christ once entered into humanity, and
enters again into each man, not only to express God's grief and pain over each man's
sin, but also that He may say in his capacity as the Son, and also as the Head of the
race, Righteous art Thou, O God, in thus
judging sin, in connecting suffering eternally with sin. In this aspect both the
capacities of Christ combine.

Another time this was the turn his conversation took : Suppose a man who had
been all his life long a reckless profligate,
sinning every day without the least com-

punction; but suppose at last it had come
to this, that he must either commit one of
his daily sins, tell one of his habitual lies,
or be put to death unless he did so. It
might be that this might pull him up; conscience might awake, check him, and keep
him from the meanness of buying his life
by one of those sins which he had been in
the habit of committing daily without scru-
ple. Here something within might whisper, Do it this once, and then you will have
time to repent of all your past life; for if
you die now you must go to hell. This
would seem to be conscience, but it would
be a false conscience. The true conscience
would say, Do it not: fear not that God can
ever punish a man for doing right, or that
a man can ever lose by doing God's will,
by obeying his own voice within him. In
every call from God to arise and do the
right, justification for the past is implied.
The justification comes contained in this
voice of conscience. The command to ab-
stain from sin implies that God justifies,
— has put away the past sin. And thus
when the man consents with his full will to
death rather than do the wrong, and recog-
nizes and accepts in the call to die God's

loving purpose towards him, he receives the
forgiveness and justification into himself.
Every call of God to do right, every voice
of conscience, is a new coming of justification to the man.   Even if it come in the
shape of a condemnation of the man's present condition, it is still the same, a fresh
inflow of justification from God.   For why
should He deal with the man at all, even
to condemn him, if He did not intend to
deliver him from sin and alienation?

When Sir Walter Raleigh was brought
to trial, the counsel for his defense pleaded
that he could not by the law of England,
or by right justice, be condemned or even
tried for the said offense, because it took
place long ago, and he had received the
royal commission to serve the Queen since
the offense had been committed.   And
every time the royal commission was given
to a man, it by its nature declared that he
was a perfectly clear, free man.   So every
time that God speaks to us in conscience,
we may accept it as declaring that He still
justifies us, pardons us, calls us to put away
our sin, to die to our own selves, to give
up our own will and enter into his will.
And if we apprehend his call thus, and do

surrender ourselves willingly to his will, we accept the justification.

Another time, during that same visit, he said: The Bible is the great interpreter of consciousness and of conscience. Conscience is not mine; I am its. Often a man does not understand his conscience. A man, for instance, is wroth with his neighbor, who has wronged him, vents his anger against him, and longs to be revenged. Another comes and says to him, Why are you angry with that man? Why do you wish to trample on him? He answers, Because my conscience, looking at this injury in God's light, tells me that I do well to be angry and revengeful against him. The other rejoins, Did God really give you this conscience, this sense of your neighbor's sin, in order that you may trample on him, or not rather that, feeling deeply his sin, you may help him out of it? Again, years afterwards, the expostulator finds the angry man on the point of death; he is overwhelmed with the remembrance of his sin, and he says that all this terror is just the effect of God's anger towards him, and the sign that He intends to punish him. The expostulator puts him in

mind of their conversation years ago, asks
him if he thinks that God has this anger,
and has made this declaration of it in his
terror-stricken conscience, that He may de-
stroy him, and not rather that He may help
him out of his sin and his terror, just as
the strong conviction of his neighbor's
wrong-doing years ago was given to himself, not that he might take vengeance on
him, but that he might help him out of his
sin.

Such were some of the lines on which his
thoughts ran during that first visit in 1854.
All who knew him will probably recognize
in him either the very thoughts they have
themselves heard from him, or at least
thoughts like those they have heard from
him. These were the channels which his
mind latterly had grooved for itself, and
which it wore ever deeper as time went on.
When he was alone with a sympathetic
hearer, and sometimes to those who were
not very sympathetic, his discourse would
return again and again to the same channels, and flow on for hours together in
thoughtful monologue.

These more inward subjects of conversation he often varied by recurring to the

events and the persons of his past life
which had most impressed him. He would
often talk with much affection of the
friends he had made abroad, at Paris, at
Geneva, and at Rome, and most frequently
recurred to the memory of Madame de
Broglie.

Of home events, that which filled the
largest place in his retrospect was the revival of religion which began at Row in
1828, and continued there till it was cut
short by the summary verdict of the General Assembly in 1831. Mr. Erskine, as is
well known, had been an earnest sympa-
thizer and fellow-worker with Mr. Campbell, had stood by his side through all the
persecutions he was called to undergo, and
had been a witness of that never-to-be-
forgotten night in the General Assembly
which cast out from the church of his fathers one of the saintliest of her sons. The
decisions of the assembly could not touch
Mr. Erskine, but all the more for this he
felt the deep wrong which the church by
that act had done to his friend, and the still
deeper injury she had done to herself. He
never ceased to regard it as the stoning by
the Church of Scotland of her best prophet,

the deliberate rejection of the highest light vouchsafed to her in his time. Few felt as he did that day; but as years went on, more and more woke up to know what an evil thing had been done in the land. From that time on for many years he ceased to have any sympathy with the Church of Scotland, when not only the men, but the truth he most prized, had been so rudely trampled down. In his eyes all the calamities that befell her were the natural sequel of, perhaps judgments for, the wrong she had done in 1831. In the last twenty years of his life he came to know and value both the character and the teaching of some of the young generation of ministers, and from time to time he attended their ministrations. His was not the spirit to feel anything like sectarian hostility to the church, though he believed it to have so deeply sinned, but he never ceased to feel righteous indignation against the wrong-doing, though not against the wrong-doers.

One story connected with this time he used to tell. It was of the Rev. William Dow, a good man, who was minister of a parish in the south of Scotland, but who, for siding with the views of Mr. Campbell of Row, was called to stand his trial before the General Assembly. On the Sunday immediately before he went to Edinburgh for his trial, being quite sure what fate awaited him, he thus addressed his country congregation : " You all know that to-morrow I leave this to go to Edinburgh, and to stand my trial before the General Assembly. And the result I know will be that I shall be turned out of my parish, and that this is the last time I shall address you as your minister. This you all know. But there is one thing about myself which you do not know, but which I will tell you. When I first came here to be your minister I found difficulty in obtaining a house in the parish to live in. There was but one house in the parish I could have, that was suitable, and that belonged to a poor widow. I went and offered a higher rent for her house than she paid. She was dispossessed, and I got the house. I put that poor woman out of her house then, and I hold it to be a righteous thing in God to put me out of my parish now."

This accepting the punishment as a righteous thing was entirely to Mr. Erskine's mind.

His friend, Mr. Campbell of Row, writes of him in 1863 : " He is very full, as has ever been his way, of the thoughts which have last taken form in his mind, and would bend everything to them ; and my work, as of old, has been to endeavor to keep before him what he may seem to me to leave out of account." This exactly describes his discourse as his friends knew it. "And would bend everything to them," that is, to the thoughts that for the time absorbed him. This was especially observable in many of the interpretations which he imposed on difficult texts of Scripture. They were exceedingly ingenious, and such as could only have occurred to a meditative and highly spiritual mind. But it often seemed as if the interpretation was born from within his own thought, rather than gathered from impartial exegesis. So strong was the heat of his cherished convictions, that before them the toughest, most obdurate text gave way, melted, and fused into the mould which his bias had framed for it. It was the characteristic of his mind to seize whatever truth it did see with a peculiar intensity of grasp. This is what Mr. Campbell in a letter of 1868 speaks of as his " tendency to reduce

many aspects of truth to one, making him
hesitate to see now the importance, not to
say the correctness, of what he once urged,
making him, indeed, appear to give up what
he once held. I do not believe that his
views have at all changed as they appear to
himself to have done." . . . This passage
seems to mark exactly the distinction between the minds of the two friends, as they
struck me when I used to see them together,
or rather perhaps when, after conversing
with one, I afterwards spoke to the other
on the same subject. Mr. Erskine, whatever truth possessed him, threw himself
wholly into it, became absorbed in it, expounded it with a gentle yet vehement eloquence, and illustrated it with a wealth of
ingenious illustration which was quite foreign to Mr. Campbell's habits of thought.
Mr. Campbell, on the other hand, even the
truths he most realized he could contem-
plate with long patience, could move round
·them, and consider them deliberately from
every side, could see them in all their bearings on other truths, and see those other
truths in their bearing on them. This pa-
tient power of balancing truths seemingly
opposed, combined with the persistent ad-

herence to his first cherished principles, contrasted strikingly with the vehemence with which Mr. Erskine flung himself on the thoughts that had once taken possession of him.

Arising perhaps out of this tendency in Mr. Erskine to be absorbed in one great truth, which he had made to overbear all other truths that opposed it, was his belief in the final restitution of all men. This seemed to him to be the only legitimate issue of the gospel. The conviction that it was so grew on him latterly, and he expressed it freely. He used to dwell much on those passages in St. Paul's epistles which seemed to him to favor this cherished belief of his. In one thing, however, Mr. Erskine was altogether unlike most of those who hold the tenets of Universalism. No man I ever knew had a deeper feeling of the exceeding evil of sin, and of the Divine necessity that sin must always be misery. His universalistic views did not in any way relax his profound sense of God's abhorrence of sin.

Any one who talked intimately with Mr. Erskine in later years could not help hearing these views put strongly before him.

Often when he urged them on me he seemed disappointed when I could not acquiesce. I used to urge that we do not know enough of the nature and possibilities of the human will to warrant us in holding that a time must come when it will yield to moral suasion which it may have resisted all through its earthly existence. Then as to the Bible, though there are some isolated texts which seem to make Mr. Erskine's way, yet Scripture, taken as a whole, speaks a quite different language. The strongest, most emphatic declarations against his views seem to be the words of our Lord himself. Therefore I shrink from all dogmatic assertions on this tremendous subject, desiring to go no farther than the words of Scripture allow, till the day comes which shall bring forth his righteousness as the noonday.

It would be no adequate representation of Mr. Erskine as he appeared among men to conceive of him as confining all his conversation to religion and theology. Yet these, no doubt, were his favorite subjects, those that lay nearest his heart; and when he met with a sympathetic listener he poured himself forth unweariedly. It was

not any mere speculations about theology,
any mere dealing through the intellect with
what is called scientific theology. That
was to him the mere outwork, the shell of
something far more inward and vital. In
that inner region that lies beyond all mere
speculation, you felt that his whole being
was absorbed, — that he was making it his
own, not with the mere understanding only,
but that his heart, conscience, and spirit
were wholly in it. And whether his listener understood all he said (for sometimes
it was hard to catch for its subtlety), and
whether he agreed with it or not (for sometimes it was novel and even startling), no
one, who could feel what spiritual-minded-
ness was, could come away from his converse without feeling that in his society
they had breathed for a while a heavenly
atmosphere. To return from it to common things and every-day talk was like
descending from the mount of vision to the
dusty highway.

It used to be a strange feeling to walk
about his place with him, wearing, as he
did, to the outward eye, the guise of a
Scottish laird, while all the while his inner
spirit, you felt, was breathing the atmos-

phere of St. John. It was something so
unlike anything you met with elsewhere in
society. The Scotland of his later years,
in his own rank, and among all the educated classes, had become more religious
than that of his early manhood. But even
at its best the tone of religious society was
unlike his. But when left alone by himself, he was a man absorbed in the thought
of God. There is a saying of Boehme's
which he loved to quote : " The element of
the bird is the air, the element of the fish
is the water, the element of the salamander
is the fire, and the heart of God is Jacob
Boehme's element." As I have heard him
quote these words I used to think, " Thou
art the man that Boehme describes himself
to be." What Mr. Alexander Scott is re-
puted to have said, many other hearts will
respond to, that ever after he knew Mr.
Erskine he never thought of God but the
thought of Mr. Erskine was not far away.
And combined with this went another tendency, — I mean the absolute conviction that
all true thought about God would be found
to harmonize with all that is truest and
highest in the conscience and the affections
of man. It was the desire of himself to see

and to make others see this harmony, to
see that Christian doctrine was that which
alone meets the cravings of heart and conscience, — it was this desire which animated
him in all the books he wrote, and in all
the many conversations he carried on.

Over the social circle that met within his
home at Linlathen, his Christian influence
showed itself in many ways, and though
differing according as it met with different
characters, yet was always in harmony with
itself. Among the many relatives of all
ages and characters who visited him, and
the guests who, especially during summer,
were welcomed to Linlathen, there were of
course those who could not sympathize with
him in his deepest interests. If, however,
they cared for literature, in Mr. Erskine
they found one who was at home in all that
was finest and most soul-like in literature,
ancient and modern, and his bright and
sympathetic remarks or questions drew out
the stores of even the most reserved. The
classics he knew and loved to speak of.
Shakespeare he knew only less well than
the Bible, and his conversation was edged
with many apt quotations from him. Even
when sportsmen were his guests, men whose

chief delights lay at Melton Mowbray, he
found some bond of sympathy with them,
something that made them take pleasure
in his society. He had a wonderful art of
setting every one at ease, and drawing out
the best side of every character. In this,
his own natural graciousness was perfectly
seconded by his sister, Mrs. Stirling, who so
long presided as the lady of the house at
Linlathen. She was of a character hardly
less remarkable than her brother, like-
minded with him in her aims and in the
spirit she was of, but with more turn for
the practical affairs of life. She stood, in
a large measure, between Mr. Erskine and
the buffets of the outward world, and allowed his life to flow on in its own natural
current. How much her presence contributed to make Linlathen the well-ordered
and happy home that it was can hardly be
overestimated. Never perhaps were brother
and sister more fitted to each other, more
able to supply what the other had not,
and so to make a home in which all the
requirements of refined Christian society
were combined. Very seldom has a home
been seen in which perfect ease, refinement, and high intelligence so blended with

the most sunny graciousness and all-pervading Christian charity. No one, however great a stranger he might be when he entered that house, could there be a stranger long; and none of the many who visited Mr. Erskine and his sister there — neighbors, high and low, guests from far and near — will ever forget it. Another element was added to the family group by his sister, Mrs. Paterson, who generally spent a great deal of the summer at Linlathen. She was so much of an invalid that she could not come down-stairs regularly, but when she was able for this, or when visitors had an opportunity of conversing with her in private, they found in her an interest in things as keen and an intelligence as active as her brother's, combined with a spirit singularly gentle, attractive, and elevating. To one looking back on the Linlathen of those years, it seems to represent the very Scottish counterpart of that gentle and high-souled English family group which is portrayed in the "Memorials of a Quiet Life."

I remember calling one summer afternoon at Mrs. Paterson's house in Morningside, about the year 1863 or 1864, I think.

Mrs. Paterson, Mrs. Stirling, and her sister-in-law Mrs. James Erskine, were alone together in the drawing-room. For an hour I sat while they talked of the things nearest their own hearts and their brother's, in a natural but most unworldly strain, such as conversation seldom attains. Mrs. Paterson perhaps spoke most, but all three took part. It was early summer, and the western sun was shedding a soft light along the green slopes of the Pentland hills, visible from the drawing-room window. When the hour was ended I came away, but a soothing sense remained long after, as though for a brief while I had been allowed to overhear a high, pure strain of heavenly music. I felt that all three were, not by natural kinship only, but by the kinship of the heart, spiritual sisters of their gifted brother.

With any of his guests at Linlathen who cared for it, Mr. Erskine used to continue his talk, not only in his library and along the corridor, but in walks about the place, or in a longer walk to the bare, bleak links of Monifieth, where the outlook was on the eastern sea. A few of his sayings during such walks recur to me.

He said more than once that all the most deeply devout men he had known had been brought up as Calvinists. "How, then, do you reconcile this fact with the life-long conflict you have maintained against Calvinism?" "In this way," he would reply: "Calvinism makes God and the thought of Him all in all, and makes the creature almost as nothing before Him. So it engenders a deep reverence, a profound humility and self-abasement, which are the true beginnings of all religion. It exalts God infinitely above the creature. In this, Calvinism is true and great, and I honor it. What I cannot accept is its conception of God as One in whom power is the paramount attribute, to which a loving righteousness is made quite subordinate, and its restriction of the love of God in a way which seems to me not righteousness, but partiality."

Another time, when speaking of how orthodoxy, correctness of intellectual belief, is made in Scotland the test and synonym of goodness, he used to tell of a gardener he had at Linlathen. The old man was, like many of his countrymen, a great theologian, and piqued himself on the correctness of his belief. One day, when speaking of the good men he had known, the gardener said, after enumerating several, "And there was Mr. Campbell of the Row; he was a vara gude man, but then he devairged [diverged]," — as if after that there was no more to be said for him.

His relations to his neighbors at Linlathen of all classes were of the kindliest. I remember hearing of his having lost a number of his best Southdown ewes which were feeding in the park. The keeper watched, and found that the destroyer was a large Newfoundland dog, which he caught in the act. The dog belonged to a resident in the neighboring town of Broughty-Ferry. The case went before the sheriff, and the owner of the dog was condemned to pay to Mr. Erskine the value of all the ewes which had been destroyed. Some time afterwards Mr. Erskine was taken with compunction, as if he had been too hard on his neighbor; so he sent him from his own flock a present of fully as many ewes as had been paid for. One never heard how this act was regarded in the district, whether as the deed of unselfish kindness that it was, or as one of eccentricity and weakness.

In earlier days of his discipleship, when he and Mr. Campbell first saw a light in God's love which not many others then acknowledged, Mr. Erskine, as is well known, had for a time expounded, and even preached, to audiences more or less large, at Linlathen and elsewhere. He had, however, long ceased to do this when I first knew him. His voice was only heard in his morning reading of the Bible, and in prayer with his own household in the library. The impression of him, as he conducted that simple worship, those who shared it will always remember. His daily walk, either in going or returning, often brought him to some cottage where a sick or aged person lay, and he would request his companion to remain for a little, while he went in to pay a friendly visit. Many records might have been gathered of persons around Linlathen, at Broughty-Ferry and elsewhere, who being in darkness and distress of mind, and finding no relief from the ministrations of the ordinary religious teachers, first found light and peace from words spoken to them by Mr. Erskine. One can readily understand how this should be. It was not only that his large

human sympathy, and his deep moral and
spiritual hold of truth, fitted him to reach
hearts that were in darkness, but it was
because, when he spoke to them of God and
his love, he did not speak, as at second-
hand, of something he had read in a book,
but he witnessed directly to that which he
had himself known and tried.

For the last ten or twelve years before
Mrs. Stirling died, he generally took a
house in Edinburgh, where he passed the
months from January to May. This suited
his social disposition, and gave him exactly
that kind of society which he most relished.
He thus was able to continue his intercourse
with such of his early companions as still
survived, with his cousin, the scholarly Mr.
George Dundas (afterwards Lord Manor),
with Lord Rutherfurd, and with the aged
Mr. James Mackenzie, son of "the Man of
Feeling." In this way, too, he saw something of younger men, who were drawn to
him by reverence and affection, and whom
he welcomed with a sympathy at once fatherly and fraternal. Those winters in Edinburgh gave him, moreover, opportunities
of seeing many relatives and friends not
easily seen at other times, and each winter

brought his two old and like-minded friends,
Mr. Duncan of Parkhill, and Mr. Campbell
(of Row), to be his guests for a time.   In
his house in Edinburgh he used to exercise
the same loving hospitality as at Linlathen.
"What is the end of all social gatherings
of men?" some one asks, and answers, "A
little conversation, high, clear, and spiritual."   This result was attained, if ever, at
the board where Mr. Erskine presided. He
used to gather round his table small parties,
seldom more than eight or ten, of persons
well assorted, who would like to meet each
other.   Never were there more delightful
evenings, — anecdote, pleasant humor, and
thought flowed freely and naturally, and
you came away feeling that the hours had
passed, not only enjoyably, but profitably.
Of a visit to Mr. Erskine in 1864, Mr.
Campbell wrote: "Mr. Erskine is so varied
and full, passing so easily to what Professor
Thomson, who dined with us yesterday, or
Professor Rogers, who dined with us to-day,
contribute from their special stores, drawing them out as an intelligent questioner
does, and often by natural transition passing to what is higher."

His forenoons were spent partly in writ-

ing letters; sometimes in giving more regular expression to his favorite thoughts;
partly, also, in reading. His love of literature was intense, with a keen sense of what
was most excellent. I have already noted
his familiarity with Shakespeare, and how
readily he drew on that great storehouse.
If you went into his sitting-room on a forenoon during these years, you would probably find him engaged in reading some of
the speeches of Thucydides, or a dialogue
of Plato. His Greek was kept in continual
exercise by the close study of the New Tes-
tament in the original. He used to say to
me that he had such a thirst for learning,
and admiration of it, that he would have
made himself a learned man had it not been
for the early failure of his eyesight. This
confined his reading for some years to a
quarter of an hour a day. What more he
overtook was by the tedious process of listening to a reader. This inability to study
cast him back on his own thoughts, and did
much to foster that inwardness of mind
which was natural to him.

During those winters his appearance, as
he passed along Princes Street to and from
his afternoon visit to the New Club, must

have struck most passers-by, — with his broad hat or wide-awake, and his quaint, antique, weather-fending guise. Walking with him on one such occasion, I observed that he stopped and spoke very cordially with a distinguished ecclesiastical leader of the time, who was well known to disagree with him, and strongly to disapprove of his views. " You seem very cordial with Dr. ——." With a smile, he answered, " He tries to cut me, but I never allow him. I always walk in before him, and make him shake hands." On another occasion, as I walked with him, we forgathered with Dr. John Brown, and we three stood talking together for some time. When Dr. Brown passed on, he said: "I like him ; he is a fine vernacular man ; he can speak to you in a whisper. Have you ever observed it is only Scotchmen who can speak in a whisper ? The English cannot do it."

One Sunday he and I had been together to church where a young divine preached a somewhat rambling, unconnected discourse. We came away, and said nothing. Some time afterwards, as we were walking in silence, he stopped, and looking round to me said, " The educated mind desiderates

a nexus," and then, without any more,
passed on.

These are small things, hardly worth repeating, but they are characteristic, and, to
those at least who knew him, may serve
to recall, not only his tone of voice, but the
quiet smile with which he used to say such
things.

Among the last of the occasions on which
he was allowed to receive his friends in Edinburgh was in the spring of 1866, when
his old and much-valued friend, Mr. Carlyle, after a long absence, revisited Edinburgh, to be installed as Rector of the University. Many will still remember the wise
and gracious courtesy with which he then
performed the duties of hospitality, on the
one hand securing for his guest the repose
he needed and desired, on the other according to as many as possible the coveted privilege of meeting the sage of Chelsea. On
the day on which Mr. Carlyle addressed the
students in the large Music Hall, Mr. Erskine, knowing how great was the effort for
a retired man of Mr. Carlyle's years, and
anxious how he might feel after it was over,
had asked no one to dinner for that day.
When the address was well achieved, and

Mr. Erskine found that Mr. Carlyle was none the worse, but rather the better for the deliverance, he asked two or three of his intimate friends to come and join a quiet dinner-party. That evening Sir William Stirling Maxwell sat at the foot of the table, and with nice tact gave such turn to the conversation as allowed fullest scope to the sage who has praised silence so well, but fortunately does not practice it. Released from his burden, Mr. Carlyle was in excellent spirits, and discoursed in his most genial mood of his old Dumfriesshire remembrances, of the fate of James IV., and other matters of Scottish history, and of the then Emperor Napoleon, of whom, as may be imagined, he was no admirer. Those days when Mr. Erskine received Mr. Carlyle as his guest were among the last of his hospitalities in Edinburgh.

During the next winter his two sisters, first Mrs. Stirling, soon after Mrs. Paterson, who had been the chief earthly supports of his life, were removed, and his house was left to him desolate. The staff of family affection, on which he had so long leaned, was broken; the hand which for years had arranged all the outward framework of his

life was withdrawn. All that was identified
with his youth, all that " his eye loved and
his heart held converse with " from childhood, had now passed out of sight. " He
was a man moving his goods into a far country, who at intervals and by portions sends
them before him, till his present abode is
well-nigh unfurnished. He had sent forward his friends on their journey, while he
himself stayed behind, that there might be
those in heaven to have thoughts of him,
to look out for him, and receive him when
his Lord should call." These words, in
which Dr. Newman describes the old age of
St. John, truly represent Mr. Erskine during those last years. Though he passed his
few remaining winters in Edinburgh, yet he
never again after Mr. Stirling's death took
a house there. In summers at Linlathen
he used to say: " As I go to bed at night
I have to pass two empty rooms, which
I never passed before without entering
them." Younger relatives gathered around
him. His nephew and niece especially, who
lived with him at Linlathen, did for him all
that the most devoted and watchful love
could do. But his own strength and health
were declining, and there was an oppression

about his heart which at times was distressing. Still, during those last years he labored on assiduously to complete a book which he had begun when roused by a strong sense of the spiritual blindness betrayed in Renan's much-talked-of "Vie de Jesus." That book, notwithstanding all its outward grace of style and felicitous description, seemed to him at the core so short-sighted and misleading that, after a silence of more than thirty years, he once more took his pen to say something in reply to it. He utterly repudiated the character which it drew of our Lord, and almost resented the fatuity which could separate with a sharp line the morality of the gospels from their doctrinal teaching as to Christ himself. He used to say: "As you see in many English churches the Apostles' Creed placed on one side of the altar, on the other the Ten Commandments, so Renan would divide as with a knife the moral precepts of the gospels from their doctrines. Those he would retain; these he would throw away. Can anything be more blind? As well might you expect the stem and leaves of a flower to flourish when you had cut away the root, as to retain the morality

of the gospels when you have discarded its
doctrinal basis. Faith in Christ, and God
in Christ, is the only root from which true
Christian morality can grow." This, or
something like this, was what he used to
say, and to bring this out fully in connec-
tion with his other views of the inner and
eternal relation of the Son to the Father,
and of the Father to the Son, was a work
which he desired to accomplish before the
end. The whole line of thought which he
wished to express stood out clear before his
own mind to the last, but the physical labor
of committing it to paper and arranging it
was great, almost too great for him. Yet
he never ceased trying to put it into shape ;
and if he died without accomplishing all
he wished to do, completed chapters were
found sufficient to appear, after his death,
in his last work, " The Spiritual Order."

The last visit which I remember having
paid to him at Linlathen was on the sixth
day of July, 1868, a beautiful summer day.
I had arrived there in the forenoon, and
after lunch he asked me to take a drive
with him. We drove to the manse of
Mains, to make his first call on a young
minister who had been recently placed

there. Mains was a parish in which he had
taken much interest, and which, chiefly
through his influence, had enjoyed the benefit of a succession of unusually good ministers. Among those whom Mr. Erskine
had helped to place there, and with whom
he had afterwards lived in much intimacy,
were the late Dr. John Robertson, afterwards of the Cathedral Church, Glasgow,
and the Rev. John M'Murtrie, now minister of St. Bernard's, Edinburgh.

It was a day of delightful sunshine, and
as we drove to Mains the genial air seemed
to touch the springs of old feeling and memory with him. He went back in retrospect
to early companions, the large cousinhood
who used to meet at Airth and Kippendavie. He said how he loved the scenery of
Stirlingshire and Perthshire, with the green-
ness and luxuriance of their woodland, —
not without, I think, a silent mental contrast with the bare landscape and stunted
timber of the eastern coast, in which his
own lot had been cast. He said, if I remember right, that he had often had a
dream of spending his last summers in
those western regions which were so dear
to him in memory.

After we had returned from our drive, we sat for some time on the lawn just over the Dighty Water, which ran underneath the bank on the top of which the house stands. It was about six o'clock P. M., and the sun was shining warm on us as we sat, and beautifying the landscape near and far. After talking for some time, he asked me if I remembered Mr. Standfast in the "Pilgrim's Progress," and his words when he came to the bank of the stream: "The thoughts of what I am going to, and of the conduct that waits for me on the other side, doth lie as a glowing coal at my heart." . . . And then, looking across the Dighty to its farther bank, he added, "I think that within a year from this, I shall be on the other side."

He then, I think, spoke of the awful silence of God, how it sometimes became oppressive, and the heart longed to hear, in answer to its cry, some audible voice. Then he quoted that word, "Be not silent to me, O Lord: lest if thou be silent to me, I become like them that go down into the pit;" and then I know he added, "But it has not always been silence to me. I have had one revelation; it is now, I am sorry to say, a matter of memory with me. It was not a revelation of anything that was new to me. After it, I did not know anything which I did not know before. But it was a joy for which one might bear any sorrow, — ' Joie, joie, pleurs de joie,' as was the title of a tract I used to read at Geneva. I felt the power of love, that God is love, that He loved me, that He had spoken to me." As he spoke he touched me quickly on the arm, as if to indicate the direct impact from on high of which he had been aware. As he walked away, leaning on my arm, round the west end of the house towards the door, he added : "I know many persons in the other world, and I would like to see them again." This was, as far as I remember, the last visit I paid him at Linlathen. The conversation I have just given was so remarkable that I made a note of it immediately, and I have given it as I wrote it down at the time.

During the next two winters (1868–69 and 1869–70) I saw him from time to time in Edinburgh.

One thing very remarkable during those last years must have struck all who conversed intimately with him, — his ever-deepening sense of the evil of sin, and the personal way in which he took this home to himself. Small things done or said years ago would come back upon him and lie on his conscience, often painfully. Things which few other men would have ever thought of again, and which when told to others would seem trifling or harmless, were grievous to him in remembrance. "I know that God has forgiven me for these things," he would say, "but I cannot forgive myself." How far this burdened sense was connected with physical oppression about the heart no one can determine. He himself would have been among the last to accept the common explanation of spiritual malady by merely bodily causes. This, however, I believe, is true, that after that great effusion of blood, which was the prelude to the end, had relieved his heart, the rest was, as Mrs. Campbell writing at the time expressed it, all peace, — love, with perfect clearness of mind. I was not privileged to see him during that solemn interval when he lay waiting for the end, and speaking words full of comfort and light to all those who were around him.

But his funeral day I remember well.

It was a calm bright day of March. The funeral prayers of the English Church were read in his own library, where he had so often prayed alone and in the family. He was laid beside his mother and the brother he so revered, in Monifieth Churchyard, which is situated on the estuary of Tay, where it broadens out to meet the ocean. The churchyard was filled with his kindred, his friends, and his neighbors, and over that place and company there seemed to rest for the time a holy calm in harmony with the saintly spirit that had departed. The thoughts of others far away were centred in that churchyard on that day.

One who had in her childhood often listened to his voice, and had since then been long an invalid confined to her room,[1] breathed from her sick-bed these touching words as she thought of that day. The image in the third verse especially, all who knew him will understand : —

[1] Miss C. Noel, daughter of his old friend, the Hon. and Rev. Gerard Noel.

ASLEEP.

MARCH 28, 1879.

Toss, ye wild waves,
  Upon the shore!
He is at rest
  For evermore.

Moan o'er the surf,
  Thou wind so drear;
Moan, sob, and wail:
  He will not hear.

Close by he lies;
  But a long sleep,
His wondrous smile
  Enchained doth keep.

Roll, thou wild sea,
  Against the shore!
He is at rest
  For evermore.

GEORGE EDWARD LYNCH COTTON, D. D.,

BISHOP OF CALCUTTA.

THERE are few things that I look back to with such pure satisfaction as the privilege of having known intimately the late G. E. L. Cotton. In trying, however, to recall those years of familiar intercourse with him, I find it hard to do so, the throng and pressure of that busy time have so jostled the incidents and blurred their outlines. It is only the total impression, for the most part, that remains.

Towards the close of 1846, by the kindness of the present Bishop of London, I went, after leaving Oxford, to Rugby, to undertake one of the masterships there. During the first few days, while I stayed as guest at the schoolhouse, Dr. Tait told me a good deal of the new life and work that lay before me, and spoke of the colleagues I should meet with.

I can still distinctly recall the way in

which he spoke of Cotton, as one whom it
might do any one good to know; whose
whole life and work were a great example.
Dr. Tait had at that time been a little
more than four years head master, and I
could see that he had formed for Cotton a
peculiar admiration and affection.

I cannot quite recall the first impression
Cotton made on me, only I think it was of
one who stood calm and self-possessed in the
midst of a great whirl of work and many
more excitable persons.

In general he received strangers quietly,
and it was not at first sight that they were
most taken by him. In due time, by our
mutual friend Bradley, we drew to each
other, and began to have walks together on
half-holidays and Saturdays. Having lately
left Oxford, I was full of views and thoughts
which were then seething there below the
surface. In these Cotton was much interested, with firm, intelligent desire to know
what way the currents were setting in the
university, and from kindly sympathy with
young men, and whatever engaged their
thoughts. In these conversations, two
things in him soon struck me: first, the
large tolerance and perfect fair-mindedness

with which he tried to understand and judge ways of thinking that were different from his own ; and, secondly, his stability, — while opening his mind to new views, he was not carried away by them. He held fast without effort by his old, fixed mooring, — those truths, few and simple, which were the roots of his being.

During those early years of our intercourse I remember a characteristic trait of his mingled humor and practical downrightness. Mr. Mill's " Political Economy " had just been published, and several of the masters agreed to read it, and discuss it together afterwards chapter by chapter. Cotton was one of these. In one walk, the early chapters on Productive and Unproductive Consumption formed topic for discussion. The truth was brought out very clearly, that all that was spent in recreation, banquets, etc., beyond what goes to invigorate body and mind for fresh productive labor, is so far wasted and a loss to the community. With most persons it would have stopped there. Cotton, partly from love of a joke, partly from his earnest practical turn, began to press this truth home. Banquets among the masters had at that

time in some quarters grown to rather large
dimensions; he urged that all banquets
should straightway be curtailed within
the limits prescribed by political economy.
This proposal to square practice by speculation caused much discussion and amusement, and gave rise to one humorous incident. The present Oxford Professor of
Political Economy may perhaps remember
these things.

Our intimacy, once begun, was ripened
into friendship by some time spent together
abroad, in the summer of 1849. We met
at Dresden, where Cotton and Mrs. Cotton
were staying, two of his sixth form pupils
accompanying them. Together we all traveled to Prague, spent some days there, and
returned to Dresden.

It would be impossible to find a more delightful traveling companion than Cotton
was. His entire unselfishness; his perfect
temper, placid and even; always interested;
the continued play of his quiet, peculiar
humor on all the little incidents and traits
of character we met with; his unwearied
love of things and places historic; the
thoroughness, the kindliness, that pervaded
all he said and did, — made his society at

once calming, strengthening, and exhilarating.

Prague, I remember, greatly charmed
him. He was struck by the Eastern look
it had, which was something new to all of
us. There was the palace and church of the
Hradschin, with its tombs of the Bohemian
kings nine centuries old; the bridge, with
its crucifix and ever-burning lamps, supported
by a fine laid on the Jews; the
mouldy synagogue, one of the earliest in
Europe; while in the shattered windows
and battered walls of the houses were
freshly seen the marks which Winditzgratz
and his Austrians had left on the town during
last year's revolution. It was the enlargement
it gave to his historic sympathies
that formed to him the greatest charm of
travel. One occurrence at Prague greatly
amused Cotton. On the first evening after
our arrival we were invited to a party
which turned out to be made up of German-hating
Czechs, the name of the Sclavonic
inhabitants of Bohemia. We had
never till that day exactly known of the existence
of this small race of Sclaves. But
that evening we found ourselves sitting with
a number of fierce, patriotic Czechs, toast-

ing in German wine "Auf die Bruderschaft
der Czech und der Engländer." While Cotton was at Rugby, each summer vacation,
sometimes the Christmas ones, too, was
laid out methodically, not merely for ease
and pleasure, but to combine needed relaxation with some increased enlargement of
his knowledge of men and of places famed
in history.

In the summer of 1850, while Cotton and
Mrs. Cotton were in Germany, he had a
severe attack of rheumatic fever, which
prevented him from returning at the usual
time to his school duties. As I had then
no boarding-house of my own, Cotton wrote
asking me to undertake the charge of his
for a time. After some weeks he was so
far recovered as to return to Rugby, still
quite unfit for work. He and Mrs. Cotton
returned for a week or two, and lived in
their own home as guests, the name and
character he insisted on assuming. After
a short stay he left again for the rest of
the half year; but I still vividly remember
with what consideration and good feeling
he carried the whole thing through, so that
he converted what might have been an em-
barrassing situation into a most friendly

and pleasant visit. During the weeks I took this charge I had an opportunity of seeing what I had always heard, the excellence of Cotton's work as head of a boarding-house. It was a house in all things well-ordered, filled with a prevailing spirit of quiet industry and cheerful duty-doing.

Good as was Cotton's work in his form, it was only in his own house that his full influence was manifest. What Arnold had been to the whole school, that Cotton was to his own house, the boarders in it, and his private pupils out of it. No two men, perhaps, were ever more different in temperament than the calm, unimpassioned Cotton and the resolute Dr. Arnold; yet notwithstanding this, of all Dr. Arnold's pupils or followers none imbibed more largely his spirit, and acted out his system more entirely, than Cotton did. The præpostors system, as Arnold conceived and recreated it, he thoroughly adopted and carried out. To get hold of his sixth form pupils, win their confidence, mould their views of life and conduct, and through them to reach and influence the younger boys, — on this idea, by which Arnold governed Rugby, Cotton threw himself with his whole heart,

and by it made his house what it was, one
of the best, not only in Rugby, but in
any public school. It was his habit to live
in great confidence and intimacy with the
præpostors in his house, and they with few
exceptions returned his confidence, and, as
far as boys could, entered into his views.
And so they were the channels by which
his mind and character reached, more or
less, every boy under his roof.

In the routine of his daily work, there
was " unresting, unhasting industry," —
method, orderly but not pedantic, each
duty done punctually and faithfully. Yet
he never seemed to be in a hurry, almost
always to have leisure.

If a boy's prose or verse copy was looked
over in his study, this was done as carefully
as a sermon to be preached in the chapel.
Some parts of a master's duty, for instance
the scratching of innumerable copies daily,
I knew to be painfully irksome to him.
Yet I often wondered with what cheerful-
ness he did these things; the pupils never
knew how irksome he felt it. For when
the work was done, he would take the opportunity of speaking a few friendly words
to the boy, and so getting to know him

better. Many men, who may try to go through these details with something like the same exactness, find themselves, when the long routine is over, so wearied out that they have no heart for further intercourse with boys, but must seek leisure or silence.

It was not so with Cotton. Whether in his study correcting exercises, or afterwards in his drawing-room, he sought every opportunity of conversing with his pupils, and showing them that he took interest in them. A laborious life of this kind leaves most men no leisure for reading. But Cotton, even in his busiest times, had generally, beside lighter reading, some solid work on hand. And from his vacations he generally came back having, along with his relaxation, mastered one or more important work, with which he had enlarged his knowledge.

The custom of reading or speaking some practical words to the boys assembled for Sunday evening prayers was in most boarding-houses occasional. With Cotton the "sermonette," as he used to call it, was almost invariably given every Sunday night. This way of teaching suited his turn, and he was a great master of it. These were not formal, like church sermons, but brief, plain, pithy words. Some part of school life and daily duty was reviewed before the boys in the light of Christian principle, and that with such plainness and directness that there was no getting past it. These, I believe, had more effect on his pupils, partly with the force with which they were put; still more, because the boys felt that they were entirely in keeping with his own life, and summoned up the spirit in which he himself lived and worked and wished them to share with him. He used to say jokingly himself, " I think that I am a shepherd, not a goatherd." By this he meant to say that it was not by throwing himself into their games, playing cricket and football with them, as some masters do, that he could influence boys. Unless there were something else in a boy than animal spirit and love of games, he felt that he could not reach him. He required some degree of thoughtfulness or some sense of duty — at least, some common sense — to be stirring in a boy before he could find a point of contact with him. If he could only be got at by his animal sympathies, Cotton felt that he was not the man for him. And so it was to their higher nature, mainly their conscience or intelligence or affection, that his character commended itself. When, however, any of these had once been touched, then they found other things in him which they had not expected. His humorous sayings, quaint remarks, and jokes were to those who knew him well, colleagues and pupils, a continual amusement.

To his house there came many pupils from the most serious homes in England. He used to say that he thought it was his calling to take boys who had been brought up in the strictest Evangelical system, and fit them for contact with the world. He endeavored to expand their minds and remove their prejudices, while he tried to confirm and deepen whatever good religious principles they had learned. If in some cases he did not succeed, if there are instances in which pupils of his have since wandered wide of their first faith, the fault was not in him or his teaching, It is but one result of that spiritual tempest which of late years has so cruelly strained young minds in the English universities, and stranded, as has been truly said, many of

the finest spirits on every shore of thought.
Of one thing I am sure, that those who
have since been led to differ from him most
widely still look back on Cotton, as they
remember him at Rugby, with undimin-
ished affection.

His house work, and the impressions he
made on his pupils, formed the centre of
Cotton's influence in Rugby. But it did
not end there : elder boys in other houses,
seeing the effect he had on his own pupils
and their attachment to him, were drawn
towards him, and welcomed any opportunity of knowing him. He thus became a
rallying point for whatever was best in the
school, and also in a great measure the up-
holder of the Arnoldian spirit in it. If in
some things, as in the stress of responsibility which it threw on the præpostors, this
spirit was overstrained, — if it pressed too
strongly the spring of " moral thoughtfulness " (the peculiar Rugbeian virtue, or vice
as some would call it), so as in some cases to
provoke an after-rebound, — Cotton, though
not unaware of this possible result, would,
I think, have said that he, notwithstanding,
accepted the system, and threw himself into
it as the best that had yet been discovered
for working public schools.

I have noticed the methodic way in which he went through each day's routine of work. Neither rapid at it nor slow, he always seemed to have each thing done at the proper time, and most days to have some leisure over, and this leisure he employed, partly in social duties, partly in reading.

He always had on hand some solid work, historical, theological, or other. This he read in the most systematic, exhaustive way, so that when he was done he could reproduce all that was most valuable in it for the information of others.

I never knew any one who could give a clearer, more well-ordered digest of anything he had read, heard, or seen; hence his knowledge, even in that busy life, every year made a steady increase.

His imagination, too, not originally, I should think, one of his strongest faculties, grew richer every year he lived. This is one of the mental gains that seemed to grow out of a moral nature true to itself. You see many a time a naturally fervid imagination divorced from moral purpose burn brightly in early youth, but grow fainter as time goes on; while the imagination in other

men, originally stiff and bald, as the meaning of life deepens to them, expands and
deepens with their years. This growth of
imaginative power is observable in Arnold's
later as compared with his earlier writings.
And I think the same was the case with
Cotton, and the cause was the same in
both. But in most other respects no two
men holding the same views, and governed
by the same aims, could be more unlike
each other.

If Cotton lacked much which Arnold
had, one thing he possessed which Arnold
wanted, — the humor that oozed from him
and gave unfailing zest to all he said.
This was closely connected with his temper, which was the most placid you would
meet with in a lifetime. I do not suppose
any one ever saw Cotton in a rage. I never
saw him even approach to being angry,
though I have seen him deeply pained on
hearing of some baseness of action or false-
ness of word.

His perfect temper arose in a large
measure from his great unselfishness. The
" heart at leisure from itself " was in him
untroubled by those feelings which spring
out of self-regard and make up most men's
annoyances.

The attachment of his elder pupils, especially the sixth form boys, to him was wonderful; not less deep were his feelings towards them. The earnest side of his character drew out their reverence, the humorous and jocular side interested and amused them. His jokes and quaint sayings were a kind of possession of all his house, and through them of the whole school.

During his vacations he visited at the homes of his elder pupils, or took them with him on his foreign travels. I well remember his return from seeing off in the train a favorite pupil, leaving school for the university, in whose future he felt a special interest. Cotton had seen much of him during his later school days, and now on the last had gone with him on the train. When Cotton returned he told me a good deal of what they had spoken about, their last words, the parting; and then he added, with a wave of his arm and the tears in his eyes (strange to see in one usually so calm), "And so passed the greatest interest I ever had in Rugby."

To this power of attaching his pupils, and through them winning the regards of others like-minded, it was that he owed his

greatest success at Marlborough. It enabled him to draw round him a band of
young masters fresh from the universities,
who went to Marlborough, not for salaries
(for these then were insignificant), nor for
the attractions of the place (for hard work
was its main attraction), but drawn solely
by love to Cotton himself, and through him
to the work he had taken in hand. That
work was to raise the then comparatively
obscure College of Marlborough out of the
depths into which it had fallen. Single-
handed, with merely average masters going
through a routine duty, he could have done
little. But he was enabled to regenerate
the school mainly by the personal magnet-
ism which attracted, and the devotion with
which he inspired, his following of young
masters, men of as good ability and as high
character as the large-salaried masters of
Harrow or Rugby, and with the first ardor
of youth on their side.

It was early in 1852 that he accepted the
headship of Marlborough. His going from
Rugby was the greatest loss it could sus-
tain. But he felt that his work there was
done, and that he could put forth fresh energy in a place which he could mould to his

own mind. That summer, just before he
went to Marlborough, he came down to Scotland and visited at my father's home. All
there, though most of them did not know
him till then, greatly relished his society, his
naturalness, his quiet drollery, his unpre-
tendingness. On Sunday, I remember, he
accompanied us to the small Presbyterian
parish church. He felt much interest in being present at this form of worship, which
was new to him, but he joined in it as naturally, and with as little constraint, as the
humblest peasant there. English clergymen when in Scotland, if they go to the
Presbyterian Church at all, are apt to do so
as if they were condescending. No doubt
they are not aware of it themselves, but
the natives are, and feel it offensive. Cotton had nothing of this about him ; indeed,
nothing was more remarkable in him than
his entire freedom from the common cleri-
cal weaknesses. About many of the most
excellent clergymen there is a sort of professional enamel which they cannot get rid
of. Those of the broad school, seeing this,
sometimes fly to the other extreme and
play the layman. They are continually, as
it were, taking off their white tie and fling-

ing it in your face. From both of these ex-
tremes Cotton was equally removed. You
could speak to him about anything, express
difference or doubt, just as if he were a layman ; indeed, with far less hesitation than
you can do with most laymen. And the
consequence was, that with all laymen his
influence was much stronger than that of
most clergymen, because they felt, in what
he said, that there was nothing professional,
but that it simply was the honest conviction
of a single-hearted, truth-loving man.

When we left my father's house, he
made me lead him through the vales of
Tweed and Yarrow. Dryburgh Abbey we
visited in the beauty of a summer morning, then Melrose and Abbotsford. In the
afternoon I took him up Tweed through
the beautiful woods of Yare to the ridge of
the hill behind it. There, pausing and looking westward, we saw beneath us the whole
course of the Yarrow, as it winds from the
lochs down through the green interlapping
hills. The westering sun was streaming
down the " bonny braes." Two nights we
stayed by still St. Mary's Lake, and all day
we wandered among the hopes and side-glens
that come into Yarrow, the Douglas Burn,

Kirkliffe, by Drylife Tower, and the rest, while I told him the traditions and ballads that still haunt the spots, and make more than half their charm. We then walked down Moffat dale, and parted at Moffat. Sometimes during this short tour, as we wandered among the green hills, Cotton would begin to discuss some difficult question of education or scholastic management. The enterprise of remodeling Marlborough, now close before him, was evidently much on his mind. After one or two conversations, I bargained that these topics should be left till we had reached our inn at night. Savoring as they did of the workday world, they seemed alien to the dreamy stillness of those green pastoral uplands. To this he readily agreed. In a letter which I received from him soon after we parted, he told me that his enjoyment in this short tour had been only second to that he had felt in seeing the two or three great world-sights of his life.

Somehow, I regret to say, I never made out a visit to him at Marlborough, though often invited. But I saw him from time to time at Rugby, when, during the holidays, he came to visit others and myself there.

After his consecration as a bishop, while he was on his last visit to Rugby, just before sailing for India, a quite unexpected occurrence brought me from Scotland to Rugby, and we there met. It was on a Sunday we were there, and I remember the impression it made on me when at the close of the evening service Cotton rose, and as bishop pronounced the benediction in that chapel where for years his voice had been so familiar. On the Sunday we saw as much of each other as we could, but of course he had many friends to see. We agreed to meet early on Monday morning, as I had to leave at eight o'clock A. M.: we met at seven o'clock in the close, walked several times up and down there, — walks we had so often paced together in former years, — then at half-past seven said farewell. As we parted he gave me a copy of his Marlborough Sermons, just then published, and below my name and his own wrote, " Rugby, Sept. 6, 1858. School close, 7.30 A. M."

After he went to India I had a letter from him every now and then, one every six months or so, till the last year or two of his life, when they intermitted. I do not

know what was the reason of this, or
whether I was to blame for neglecting to
answer him.   Most pleasant, friendly, in-
structive letters they were, full of the facts
and thoughts you wished to know, told in
the clearest, most orderly, and often quaint
way.   He had more the gift of the real old
letter-writer than any one else one knows
nowadays.

In his letters he expressed himself almost
as fully as one can conceive it done, — his
life, the things he was doing, the books he
was reading, the thoughts he was most engaged in at the time he wrote.

In thinking of Cotton as he was, the
thing that most comes back on me is his
entire truthfulness and goodness: the love
of all that was good, the open conscience
toward all that was right, amounted in him
to a kind of genial goodness.

Whatever other talents and faculties he
possessed, this the central moral power in
him at least doubled his other powers.   He
was, I think, the most candid man I ever
knew; he was almost the only man I have
met who, if anything he said or did was
objected to, would not try in the least to
defend himself, but would hold up himself

and his action in the light of unbiased
reason, and judge it with strict impartial-
ity, as if it were the case of a third person.
If after consideration he was convinced that
the objection was true, he would at once
get himself to correct his view, and con-
form his thought and word and deed to his
new correction.

Another side of the same quality was his
love of truth in all its aspects, his desire to
know the best attained truth in all matters,
and ever to be increasing his knowledge of
it. Whether the matter were fact of history, or political opinion, or interpretation
of Scripture, or philosophical question, or
truth of theology, in all alike he used con-
scientiously the best helps within his reach,
strove to attain the best light extant, and
then to turn it to practical account. But
the first thing he sought was to know what
was true.

With him, however, the end of this
search was not speculative knowledge. He
desired to know that he might be and do.
The open eye for truth and knowledge min-
istered to the love of goodness, — Christian
goodness, — and all the truth he saw he
used in the service of the goodness he loved.

He had no jealousy lest the one should hurt the other, convinced that at the bottom they were in perfect harmony. So well balanced were these two habits in him that no access of fresh critical knowledge ever weakened his heart's hold on its fundamental moorings, nor did his firm hold of these narrow his mind against perceiving any new truth that might be presented to him. Indeed, while he continued to the last to be interested in all the critical and theological questions of the time, his faith in those great evangelic truths with which he began life was growing every year till its close. For speculation as an end in itself he had no caring. His strong love of practical goodness kept his thoughts solid and healthful.

He was eminently a friendly man, and one whom friends only could know. Mere acquaintances were very likely not to know or to misunderstand him. His plain, undemonstrative manner often disappointed persons on first seeing him, when they had heard much of him beforehand. You required to get beyond mere acquaintance, and within the range of intimacy, before you got a glimpse of the real man; but

then every step you took within that
range revealed his true worth more fully.
Under that calm (what strangers sometimes thought cold) exterior you found one
of the truest, most devoted hearts that ever
beat. Steadfast and devoted he was to
his friends, whether those of his own or a
younger generation, and of such friends no
one had more ; devoted to his duty whatever it was, and to the good of the place
wherever it might be in which his work
lay, yet without the narrowness or unsocia-
bleness that often accompany strict duty-
doing ; devoted to the not romantically but
to the morally heroic, in whatever form he
perceived it ; devoted to the memory of Dr.
Arnold as the best earthly embodiment of
this whom he had known. But all these
forms of human affection were deepened
and hallowed by a more central, all-pervading devotion still,—devotion to that Divine Master whom with his whole heart he
loved.

Of this central affection he seldom spoke :
it expressed itself in his life far better than
in his words. But no one could know him
without knowing that this was the strongest power within him, — that which moved

his whole being. What made it more remarkable was that it excited, in a nature
which was so entirely unexcitable, a heart
which had fervor to give, not to small or
transient things, but only to the most important. All the more concentrated was
the devotion it gave to these. Those who
knew these qualities in Cotton at Rugby
were quite prepared to see the good and
arduous work he achieved at Marlborough.
They had seen in him a singleness of eye
and a concentration of aim which doubled
all his natural powers, and drew forth ever-
new reserves of power to meet each new
emergency as it arose.

Therefore they were not surprised when
they heard how steadily and surely his influence in India grew, and how by sheer
dint of Christian character he had come to
be the acknowledged head, not of the An-
glican Church only, but of all the Christian churches in that empire.

They were prepared to hear that all laymen, as well as all ministers of every communion, looked up to him as one of the
best of all bishops, because they had known
him long since to be one of the best of
men.

DR. JOHN BROWN.

[IN MEMORIAM.]

EARLY in the morning of Thursday, May 11, 1882, Edinburgh lost its best-known and best-loved citizen, Scotland her son of finest genius, and thousands, wherever the English language is spoken, one towards whom, though they had never seen his face, they felt as to a friend. Dr. John Brown had fulfilled the appointed three-score years and ten, and had entered on his seventy-second year, before the end came. He was descended from a long and remarkable line of Presbyterian ministers of the Seceding Church, his father, grandfather, and great-grandfather being all men of a stamp rare in any church. He was, as he himself used to say, "a Biggar callant" (boy), his birthplace being that remote village, where his father had his first charge, Biggar lying alone amid its dusky moors, and looking toward the Border hills. His childhood was passed within daily sight

of Culter Fell and Kingledoors ranges,
and almost within hearing of the Tweed.
Though he went to Edinburgh at an early
age, when his father was removed to an important charge there, the lonely moorlands
and the meek pastoral hills hung about
him throughout life, and colored all his
thoughts. Theirs was the scenery he always
turned to with most affection, and their
grave, stalwart shepherds, " with their long,
swinging stride," were especially dear to
him. These scenes laid in the first ground-
colors, and Edinburgh wove the threads
they dyed into warp and woof. His youth,
manhood, and age were spent in Edinburgh,
to which he gave the fullness of his active
powers and interests. With most parts of
Scotland he became familiar, and entered
into their local traditions and peculiarities
with characteristic zeal and insight. Rare
and brief visits to London, and short Continental tours, made up all his experience
to the south of the Tweed. When his
medical education was nearly completed,
he apprenticed himself to the famous sur-
geon, the late Professor Syme, whose
character he has more than once depicted.
From first to last, he gave to that grave,

peremptory man, his revered teacher, —
who, as he was wont to say, "never wasted
a drop of ink or of blood," — an amount of
faithful love such as few men can give.
Entering life as a physician, Dr. Brown in
time obtained a practice, moderate in
range, but of a peculiar kind. To each
family which he attended he could not
come merely as a medical functionary, feeling their pulses and writing out prescrip-
tions; but he must visit them as a friend,
entering into their joys, their cares, and
their sorrows, and giving them the full
sympathy of his most tender heart. To
his patients this was soothing and delightful; but to himself it involved a heavy
draught on his sensitive spirit. When to
any of these families calamity or death
came, he took it home to himself as a
domestic affliction. But even when most
sorely tried, he kept his troubles to himself,
and gave the world his sunshine. As he
left his house and walked along Princes
Street, with nods and greetings, his presence was felt like a passing sunbeam by old
and young alike. When he entered a room
where a conclave of grave directors were
met for business, each cased in that armor

of self-defense and vigilance which men on such occasions will put on, at one remark from Dr. Brown, in which good sense, kindliness, and humor were blended, the armor of priggishness fell off, — one touch of nature had made all kin, — and they went about the work in hand restored to their natural selves. No house he visited but the humblest servant there knew him, and for each there was a gentle look or a kind word of recognition, touched with humor. When some wanderers entered a retired moorland farmhouse to see the Covenanting banner that had waved at Bothwell Brig, at first there were reserve and suspicion, till one genial word from Dr. Brown, followed by the discovery that this was he who wrote "Rab and his Friends," set all right, and the reserve at once gave place to rejoicing hospitality.

An altogether peculiar and delightful personality, a nature in which the elements were most kindly mixed, a spirit finely touched and to fine issues, — all this his familiar circle had long known, but the world did not know it till Dr. Brown had reached his eight-and-fortieth year. Then the appearance of "Rab and his Friends"

revealed it. Men and women everywhere
were thrilled as they had never been
before: few could read it dry-eyed, even
when alone ; hard-nerved must they be who
would venture to read it aloud. Brief as
the story is, and simple in its outline, it was
felt that Scotland had produced nothing like
it, nothing so full of pure, pathetic genius,
since the pen dropped from the hand of
Scott. So long — nearly fifty years — he
had kept silence, observing, reading, thinking, feeling, but speaking no word in print.
Like a still mountain loch, on a calm autumn
day, that receives into its bosom the surrounding hills, pearly clouds, and blue sky,
and renders all back more beautiful than
they are, his mind had been taking in all the
influences of nature, all impressions of men
and manners that he saw, and of the finest
poetry and literature that he read, and now
the time was come that he must reproduce
something of these, mellowed and refined
by his own beautifying personality. His
writings have been said to be egotistic.
There is not a word of egotism in them;
but they are pervaded by the writer's
personality, as all the finest literature is.
Indeed, this is that which distinguishes liter-

ature from mere information and science,
and lends to it its chief charm. Egotism
fills a man with thoughts about himself
The personality which is present in Dr.
Brown's works is full of thoughts and
sympathy for others; it has a magic touch
which makes him free to hearts and affections most unlike his own. He had, beyond
other men, that true insight which sympathy gives. Keenly discriminative of
character, he read the men he met to their
inmost core, but with such forbearance,
such large charity, that, though he saw
clearly their foibles and faults, he took hold
of these on the kindly side, saw the humor-
ousness of them, passed them by, if possible,
with a joke, and was not stirred to hatred
or satire.

This personality, which was the charm
alike of his society and of his books, would
have lain unknown to all save a few friends,
had he not been gifted with that fine literary expression which enabled him to diffuse
it abroad, to the delight of his fellow-men,
from the highest to the lowliest. No need
to regret that his writings are merely occasional, brief essays and sketches of character, and that he did not concentrate his

powers on some large work. They are such as his nature prompted and his circumstances allowed, the result of leisure hours snatched from a busy life, the overflow of his genuine self. They thus escape the formality and sense of effort that beset big books, the work of men whose trade is literature. Indeed, how much of the best literature of England has been thrown off by busy, professional men, in their few spare hours! As they stand, those three volumes, which now contain all that he has left to the world, embalm whatever has been best in the life of Scotland during the last half century. Whatever was most worth knowing in the Scotland of his time he knew, — he had seen Scott, knew Chalmers, was the friend of Thomas Erskine of Linlathen, and received his last words; was familiar with Thackeray, Dean Stanley, and with Mr. Ruskin. Vernacular as his writings are, full of local incident and coloring, they are, at the same time, as broad and catholic as humanity. Whatever there was of beauty, or nobleness, or truth anywhere, he freely welcomed it. His strong love of home and country had nothing exclusive in it, but only made him more open to under-

stand and feel with all men. He seemed
to have in himself the key to all the arts.
Painting and music, too, as in his " Halle's
Recital," were regions familiar to him.
His criticisms on these go to the quick, to
use a phrase of his own. As for poetry,
in everything but the accomplishment of
verse he was a poet born. Had he acquired
this art in youth, his exquisite feeling for
language, and his fine ear for melody of
words, would have made him one of the
most genuine of poets. Some of his brief
sketches, as " Queen Mary's Child Garden "
or " Minchmoor," and many passages inlaid
in his essays, are small prose poems.

It may easily be imagined that **Dr.**
Brown, though natural piety kept him to
the church and the politics of his fathers,
instinctively stood aloof from all controversy, political or ecclesiastical. These
matters he left to men of another mould.
His was too fine a nature, too wide, too
sympathetic, to be confined within any
bounds of politics or sect. His friendships
overwent all such limits, and included men
of every party and church. But the race
of divines from which he came left with
him their goodness, and nothing of narrow-

ness. It has been said — and there is, perhaps, some truth in the saying — that Scotchmen who have been nurtured in the national Calvinism, when they afterwards take in modern thought and literature, are apt to throw overboard the whole of their early teaching, and to be left without faith. And the reason given for this is, that the system is so inexpansive that, like cast-iron, it will break, but not bend. It was not so with Dr. Brown. The darker features of the ancestral creed, no doubt, fell into the shade, but the essence remained. A strong background of reverence, devoutness, and humble trust in God and Christ were the support of his life.

Some years ago his health declined, and he retired in a great measure from active practice and public life, and lived only in the society of his more immediate friends. These observed that, as life went on, he grew more than ever meek, humble, and contrite. During the last eight months, his health seemed to improve, and he interested himself much in a reissue of his works, adding new touches to them to within a month of his death. He did not covet the praise of authorship, but he highly prized the sym-

pathy of his fellow-men ; and the reception
which his third volume — in some ways the
most vivid and characteristic — met with
greatly pleased him.   His last illness — an
attack of pleurisy — was only of five days'
duration, and the end came to him as he
would have wished it to come, surrounded
by those he most loved, with his powers
entire to the last, and waiting the change
in peace.

While he lived, his was a reconciling spirit
wherever he went, — healing to the spirits
not less than to the bodies of men.   Would
that the country he loved so well, rent as it
is by discords, political and ecclesiastical,
might, while it laments his loss, drink in
more of his gentle and loving spirit !   How
many now mourn, and long may mourn
him, and cherish his pure memory as one of
their dearest possessions !   The most delightful companion, the most sympathetic
friend, one of the sweetest spirits of the
sons of men, —

"Oh, blessed are they who live and die like him,
Loved with such love, and with such sorrow mourned !"

NORMAN MACLEOD.

[WHEN I went to Glagsow in 1836]
Norman was a young divinity student, and
had nearly completed his course in Glasgow College. To him his father committed the entire care of the three young
men who lived in his house, and it was arranged that I, living with his aunts, should
be added as a fourth charge. This I look
back to as one of the happiest things that
befell me during all my early life. Norman
was then in the very heyday of hope, energy, and young genius. There was not a
fine quality which he afterwards displayed
which did not then make itself seen and
felt by his friends; and that youthfulness
of spirit, which was to the last so delightful, had a peculiar charm then, when it was
set off by all the personal attractions of two
or three and twenty.

His training had not been merely the
ordinary one of a lad from a Scotch manse,

who had attended classes in Glasgow
and Edinburgh Universities. His broad
and sympathetic spirit had a far richer
background to draw upon. It was Mor-
ven and the Sound of Mull, the legends
of Skye and Dunvegan, and the shore of
Kintyre, that had dyed the first and inmost
feelings of childhood with their deep
coloring. Then, as boyhood passed into
manhood, came his sojourn among York-
shire squires, his visit to Germany, and all
the stimulating society of Weimar, on
which still rested the spirit of the lately-
departed Goethe. All these things, so unlike the commonplace experience of many,
had added to his nature a variety and
compass which seemed so wonderful compared with that of most young men around
him. Child of nature as he was, this
variety of experience had stimulated and
enlarged nature in him, not overlaid it.

There were many bonds of sympathy
between us, to begin with. First, there
was his purely Highland and Celtic blood
and upbringing; and I, both from my
mother's and paternal grandmother's side,
had Celtic blood. The shores of Argyle-
shire were common ground to us. The

same places and the same people, many
of them, were familiar to his childhood
and to mine. And he and his father and
mother used to stimulate my love for that
western land by endless stories, legends,
histories, jests, allusions, brought from
thence. It was to him, as to me, the
region of poetry, of romance, adventure,
mystery, gladness, and sadness infinite.
Here was a great background of common
interest, which made us feel as old friends
at first sight. Indeed, I never remember
the time when I felt the least a stranger
to Norman. Secondly, besides this, I soon
found that our likings for the poets were
the same. Especially were we at one in our
common devotion to one, to us the chief of
poets.

I well remember those first evenings we
used to spend together in Glasgow. I went
to No. 9 Bath Street: oftener Norman would
come over to my room to look after my
studies. I was attending Professor Bu-
chanan's class, — "Bob," as we then irrev-
erently called him, — and Norman came to
see how I had taken my logic notes, and
prepared my essay or other work for next
day. After a short time spent in looking

over the notes of lecture or the essay, Norman would say, "I see you understand all about it; come, let 's turn to Billy." That was his familiar name for Wordsworth, the poet of his soul.

Before coming to Glasgow, I had come upon Wordsworth, and in large measure taken him to heart. Norman had for some years done the same. Our sympathy in this became an immense bond of union. The admiration and study of Wordsworth were not then what they afterwards became, — a part of the discipline of every educated man. Those who really cared for him in Scotland might, I believe, have then been counted by units. Not a professor in Glasgow University at that time ever alluded to him. Those, therefore, who read him in solitude, if they met another to whom they could open their mind on the subject, were bound to each other by a very inward chord of sympathy. I wish I could recall what we then felt, as on those evenings we read or chanted the great lines we already knew, or shouted for joy at coming on some new passage which was a delightful surprise. Often as we walked out on winter nights to college for some meeting of the

Peel Club, or other excitement, he would look up into the clear moonlight, and repeat : —

> " The moon doth with delight
> Look round her when the heavens are bare ;
> Waters on a starry night
> Are beautiful and fair."

Numbers of the finest passages we had by heart, and would repeat to each other endlessly. I verily believe that Wordsworth did more for Norman, penetrated more deeply and vitally into him, purifying and elevating his thoughts and feelings at their fountain-head, than any other voice of uninspired man, living or dead. Second only to Wordsworth, Coleridge was, of modern poets, our great favorite. Those poems of his, and special passages which have since become familiar to all, were then little known in Scotland, and had to us all the charm of a newly discovered country. We began then, too, to have dealings with his philosophy, which we found much more to our mind than the authorities then in vogue in Glasgow College, — the prosaic Reid and the long-winded Thomas Brown.

Long years afterwards, whenever I took up a Scotch newspaper, if my eye fell on a

quotation from Wordsworth or Coleridge,
" Here 's Norman," I would say ; and on
looking more carefully I would be sure to
find that it was he, — quoting in one of his
speeches one of the favorite lines of Glasgow days. Norman was not much of a
classical scholar ; Homer, Virgil, and the
rest were not much to him. But I often
thought that, if he had known them ever so
well in a scholarly way, they never would
have done for him what Wordsworth did, —
would never have so entered into his secret
being, and become a part of his very self.
Besides Wordsworth and Coleridge, there
were two other poets who were continually
on his lips. Goethe was then much to
him, for he was bound up in all his recent
Weimar reminiscences ; but I think that,
as life went on, Goethe, with his artistic iso-
lation, grew less and less to him. Shakespeare, on the other hand, was then, and
always continued to be, an unfailing re-
source. Many of the characters he used to
read and dilate upon with wonderfully
realizing power. Falstaff was especially
dear to him. He read Falstaff's speeches,
or rather acted them, as I have never heard
any other man do. He entered into the

very heart of the character, and reproduced the fat old man's humor to the very life.

These early sympathies, no doubt, made our friendship more rapid and deep. But it did not need any such bonds to make a young man take at once to Norman. To see him, hear him, converse with him, was enough. He was then overflowing with generous, ardent, contagious impulse. Brimful of imagination, sympathy, buoyancy, humor, drollery, and affectionateness, I never knew any one who contained in himself so large and varied an armful of the humanities. Himself a very child of nature, he touched nature and human life at every point. There was nothing human that was without interest for him; nothing great or noble to which his heart did not leap up instinctively. In those days what Hazlitt says of Coleridge was true of him: "He talked on forever, and you wished to hear him talk on forever." Since that day I have met and known intimately a good many men more or less remarkable and original. Some of them were stronger on this one side, some on that, than Norman; but not one of all contained in himself such a variety of gifts and qualities, such elasticity, such boundless fertility of pure nature, apart from all he got from books or culture.

On his intellectual side, imagination and humor were his strongest qualities, both of them working on a broad base of common sense and knowledge of human nature. On the moral side, sympathy, intense sympathy, with all humanity, was the most manifest, with a fine aspiration that hated the mean and the selfish, and went out to whatever things were most worthy of a man's love. Deep affectionateness to family and friends, — affection that could not bear coldness or stiff reserve, but longed to love and to be loved; and if there was in it a touch of the old Highland clannishness, one did not like it the less for that.

His appearance as he then was is somewhat difficult to recall, as the image of it mingles with what he was when we last saw his face, worn and lined with care, labor, and sickness. He was stout for a man so young, or rather, I should say, only robust, yet vigorous and active in figure, his face as full of meaning as any face I ever looked on, with a fine health in his cheeks, as of the heather bloom; his broad, not high brow, smooth without a wrinkle, and his mouth firm and expressive, without those lines and wreaths it afterwards had; his dark brown, glossy hair in masses over his brow. Altogether he was, though not so handsome a man as his father at his age must have been, yet a face and figure as expressive of genius, strength, and buoyancy as I ever looked upon. Boundless healthfulness and hopefulness looked out from every feature.

It was only a few weeks after my first meeting with Norman that he, while still a student, made his first public appearance. This was at the famous Peel Banquet held in Glasgow in January, 1837.

The students at the University, after rejecting Sir Walter Scott and choosing a succession of Whig rectors, had now, very much through Norman's influence, been brought to a better mind, and had elected the great Conservative leader. He came down and gave his well-known address to the students in the hall of the now vanished college. But more memorable still was the speech which he delivered at the banquet given to him by the citizens of Glasgow and the inhabitants of the West of Scotland.

It was a great gathering. I know not if
any gathering equal to it has since taken
place in Glasgow. It marked the rallying
of the Conservative party after their dis-
comfiture by the Reform Bill of 1832.

Peel, in a speech of between two and
three hours' length, expounded, not only to
Glasgow, but to the empire, his whole view
of the political situation, and his own future
policy. It was a memorable speech, I believe, though I was too much of a boy either
to know or care much about it. Many other
good speeches were that night delivered, and
among them a very felicitous acknowledgment by Dr. Macleod, of St. Columba, of the
toast, "The Church of Scotland." But all
who still remember that night will recall as
not the least striking event of the evening
the way in which Norman returned thanks
for the toast of the students of Glasgow
University. I think I can see him now,
standing forth prominently, conspicuous to
the whole vast assemblage, his dark hair,
glossy as a black cock's wing, massed over
his forehead, the " purple hue " of youth on
his cheek. They said he trembled inwardly,
but there was no sign of tremor or nervous-
ness in his look. As if roused by the sight

of the great multitude gazing on him, he
stood forth, sympathizing himself with all
who listened, and confident that they sympathized with him and with those for whom
he spoke. His speech was short, plain,
natural, modest, with no attempt to say fine
things. Full of good sense and good taste,
every word was to the point, every sentence
went home. Many another might have
written as good a speech, but I doubt
whether any young man then in Scotland
could have spoken it so well. From his
countenance, bearing, and rich, sweet voice,
the words took another meaning to the ear
than they had when read by the eye. Peel
himself, a man not too easily moved, was
said to have been greatly impressed by the
young man's utterance, and to have spoken
of it to his father. And well he might be.
Of all Norman's subsequent speeches, — on
platform, in pulpit, in banquet, and in
assembly, — no one was more entirely successful than that first simple speech at the
Peel Banquet.

During the session that followed the
banquet, the Peel Club, which had been
raised among the students to carry Peel's
election, and to perpetuate his then prin-

ciples, was in full swing, and Norman was the soul of it. Many an evening I went to its meetings in college, not as caring for its dry minutes of business, but to hear the hearty and heart-stirring impromptu addresses with which Norman animated all that had else been commonplace. There are not many remaining who shared those evenings, and those who do remain are widely scattered; but they must look back to them as among the most vivid and high-spirited meetings they ever took part in. What a contrast to the dull routine of meetings they have since had to submit to! And the thing that made them so different was Norman's presence there.

But if these first public appearances were brilliant, still more delightful was private intercourse with him as he bore himself in his home. His father had such entire confidence in him, not unmingled with fatherly pride, that he intrusted everything to him. The three boarders were entirely under Norman's care, and he so dealt with them that the tutor or teacher entirely disappeared in the friend and elder brother of all, and of each individually. Each had a bedroom to himself, in which his studies

were carried on; but all met in a common
sitting-room, which Norman named "The
Coffee-room." There, when college work
was over, sometimes before it was over, or
even well begun, we would gather round
him, and with story, joke, song, readings
from some favorite author, — Sir Thomas
Browne's "Religio Medici," Jeremy Taylor,
or some recitation of poetry, — he would
make our hearts leap up.

What evenings I have seen in that
" Coffee-room " ! — Norman, in the gray-
blue duffel dressing-gown, in which he then
studied, with smoking-cap on his head,
coming forth from his own reading-den to
refresh himself, and cheer us, by a brief
bright quarter of an hour's talk. He was
the centre of that small circle, and whenever he appeared, even if there was dull-
ness before, life and joy broke forth At
the close of the first session — I speak of
1836–37 — the party that gathered in the
Coffee-room changed. MacConochie and
Nairne went, and did not return; William
Clerk remained; and the vacant places
were, at the beginning of next session,
1837–38, filled by Robert (now Sir Robert)
Dalyell of Binns, James Horne, and John

Mackintosh, the youngest son of Mackintosh of Geddes. There were also two or three other students, who boarded elsewhere, but who were often admitted as visitors to the joyous gatherings in the Coffee-room.

Among these was Henry A. Douglas, afterwards Bishop of Bombay. While all these young friends so loved and admired Norman that it would be hard to say who did so most, — a love which he seemed to return almost equally to all, — John Mackintosh was no doubt the one who laid the deepest hold on his heart. They were fitted each to each by the complement of the other. The serious, devout, pure nature of John Mackintosh drew forth from Norman reverence more than an elder usually accords to a younger friend; on the other hand, Norman's deep and manly love of goodness and holiness won John's confidence, while his hopeful aspiration and joyousness did much to temper the tone of John's piety, which verged somewhat on austerity. I believe that their characters, so different, yet so adapted to respond to each other, were both of them much benefited by the friendship then begun.

John Mackintosh had at that time another friend, who was also his tutor, William Burns, who soon became the great revival preacher, and afterwards the missionary to China. Between Norman and William Burns, John used to live half-way in spirit. But I don't think that Norman and Burns ever knew each other intimately. Norman's mirth seemed to Burns profanity, and Burns' rapt Calvinistic piety, that looked on laughter as sinful, seemed to Norman somewhat too severe. In fact, they were not then fitted to understand each other. It was in this session of 1837–38 that the friendship of Norman with John, so fruitful in results to both, first began. He himself was not then a student, as he had received license in May, 1837, and was ordained in Loudoun in March, 1838; but until he settled in his parish he continued under his father's roof, and in the same relationship as formerly with the young men who wintered there. The church was then being greatly exercised by those contentions which ended four years afterwards in the Disruption. Norman took a lively interest in these; but from the first, both from temperament and family tradition, sided with the party who opposed the Non-Intrusionists. Not that Norman was in any measure fitted by nature to be a Moderate of the accepted type. His ardent and enthusiastic temperament could never have allowed him to belong to the party. But in the aims and contendings of the Veto men, he seemed from the first to discern the presence of sacerdotal pretensions which he his whole life long stoutly withstood.

Before the close of the session of 1837–38 Norman was appointed to the parish of Loudoun, in Ayrshire, and ordained as its minister. When the close of our next and last session in Glasgow (1838–39) arrived, he arranged that his old friends of the Coffee-room should go down and pay him a visit in his manse at Loudoun on the first of May. The usual winding-up of college had taken place in the morning, and by the afternoon a merry party were seated on the top of the Ayrshire coach, making their way through the pleasant country of Mearns, in Ayrshire, towards their friend's manse. That party consisted of William Clerk, Robert Dalyell, Henry Douglas, and myself. For some reason or other, which I cannot

now remember, John Mackintosh could not
join the party. It was a beautiful spring
evening, and the green burn braes, as we
wound along, laughed on us with their
galaxies of primroses. You may imagine
what a welcome we received when at evening we reached the manse door. We stayed
there three days, or four. The weather
was spring-like and delightful. We wandered by the side of the Irvine Water, and
under the woods, all about Loudoun Castle,
and Norman was, as of old, the soul of the
party. He recurred to his old Glasgow
stories, or told us new ones derived from
his brief experience of the Ayrshire people, in whom, and in their characters, he
was already deeply interested. All day we
spent out of doors, and as we lay, in that
balmy weather, on the banks or under the
shade of the newly budding trees, converse
more hearty it would be impossible to conceive. And yet there was beneath it an
undertone of sadness; for we foreboded too
surely, what actually has been fulfilled,
that it was our last meeting; that they who
met there would never again all meet
together on earth. There were, with the
host, five in that Loudoun party. I do not

think that more than two of them have since met at one time.

On the last day of our wanderings Norman, who had hitherto kept up our spirits, and never allowed a word of sadness to mar the mirth, at last said suddenly, as we were reclining in one of the Loudoun Castle woods: "Now, friends, this is the last time we shall all meet together; I know that well. Let us have a memorial of our meeting. Yonder are a number of primrose bushes. Each of you take up one root with his own hands; I will do the same; and we shall plant them at the manse in remembrance of this day." So we each did, and carried home each his own primrose bush. When we reached the manse, Norman chose a place where we should plant them side by side. It was all simple and natural, yet a pathetic and memorable close of that delightful early time.

Early next morning we left the manse, and I believe not one of us ever returned. It was as Norman said. We went our several ways, — one to Cambridge, two to Oxford; but never again did more than two of us foregather.

Two things strike me especially in looking

back on Norman as he then was. The first
was his joyousness, — the exuberance of his
joy, — joy combined with purity of heart.
We had never known any one who took a
serious view of life, and was really religious,
who combined with it so much hearty hopefulness. He was happy in himself, and
made all others happy with whom he had
to do. At least, they must have been very
morose persons indeed who were insensible
to the contagion of his gladness. The
second was the power, and vividness, and
activity of his imagination. He was at
that time "of imagination all compact." I
have since that time known several men
whom the world has regarded as poets ; but
I never knew any one who contained in
himself so large a mass of the pure ore of
poetry. I have sometimes thought that he
had then imagination enough to have furnished forth half-a-dozen poets. Wordsworth's saying is well known —

> " Oh, many are the poets that are sown
> By nature, — men endowed with highest gifts,
> The vision and the faculty divine,
> Yet wanting the accomplishment of verse."

Coleridge, I think, has questioned this. But
if Wordsworth's words are, as I believe they

are, true, then Norman was preëminently a poet. He had the innate power, but he wanted the outward accomplishment of verse. Not that he wanted it altogether, but he had not in early youth cultivated it; and when manhood came, the press of other and more practical duties never left him time to do more than dash off a verse or two, as it rose spontaneously to his lips. Had he had the time and the will to devote himself to poetry with that devotion which alone insures success, it was in him, I believe, to have been one of the highest poets of our time. Often during an evening in his study, or in a summer's day saunter with him by a Highland loch, I have heard him pour forth the substance of what might have been made a great original creation, — thoughts, images, descriptions, ranging through all the scale, from the sublime to the humorous and the droll; which, if gathered up, and put into the outward shape of poetry, would have been a noble poem. But he felt that he was called to do other work, and it was well that he obeyed the call as he did, and cast back no regretful look to the poetry that he might have created.

JOHN MACLEOD CAMPBELL.

[LETTER TO DR. CAMPBELL'S SON, THE REV. DONALD CAMPBELL.]

FROM early days in our family the name of Mr. Campbell of the Row was familiar. At that time, the fourth decade of this century, "The Row Heresy," as it was then called, was everywhere spoken against. But through some members of the Stirling of Kippendavie family, who used to visit in our immediate neighborhood, and who were devoted to your father and his teaching, sermons and addresses by him and his friends found their way into our household. They were read by some, and produced their own impression; and that was, that, however they might be discountenanced by the authorized teachers of the day, they contained something more spiritual, and more appealing to the spirit, than was at all common at that time. One small book that was especially valued was "Fragments of Exposition," which contained notes taken of discourses delivered by your father after he left the Church of Scotland. I well remember, about the years 1845 and 1846, at Oxford, after having heard and read a good many of Mr. Newman's sermons, and being much impressed by them, turning to this small book of your father's discourses. Though they came from a different quarter of the doctrinal heavens, and had no magic in their language as Mr. Newman's have, yet they seemed as full of spirituality, and that perhaps more simple and direct. They seemed equally removed from the old orthodoxy of Scotland, and from the spiritual teaching of the best Oxford men, confined as that was within a sacerdotal fence. Perhaps I do not rightly express it, but I remember very well how soothingly many of his thoughts fell on me during those years.

Again, when I used to visit Norman Macleod at Dalkeith, during the years from 1843 till 1850, he always talked much of your father, and of the refreshment of spirit he found in converse with him. For during those years Norman was very isolated and lonely in his church relations. He groaned in spirit over the deadness and want of

sympathy of those who had remained within
the Establishment, and of course he could
not find sympathy in those who had left it.
Your father's visits to him from time to
time were then his chief human support.

It was when Norman went to the Barony
Church, Glasgow, that, on visits to him, I
first met your father. All that I saw of him
and heard him say, during those interviews,
was in full harmony with what I had been
led to expect. But as there were always
three of us present at those times, I had no
opportunity of conversing with him alone.
After I came to St. Andrews, and began to
visit the late Mr. Erskine at Linlathen and
in Edinburgh, he, too, spoke even more of
Mr. Campbell than Norman Macleod had
done. Often he would revert to the time
of their first acquaintance, and tell me
about their experiences then.

In one visit to Mr. Erskine, at 16 Char-
lotte Square, I had a quiet hour of talk
with your father on Sunday, March 11,
1860. Of this conversation I made the
following notes shortly after : —

With regard to the realizing a continual
sense of God's Fatherhood and immediate
presence, which he so urged as the great

practical support for right living and right doing, he was asked : —

" Is not this something which a man may realize in his chamber, on his knees; but can he bear it with him into the busy world? Will this sense not be scared away by the noise of the market and the exchange?"

He said: "No doubt it is a narrow way to walk in, this, — to do all our business actively, and yet while doing it to feel that it is the business our Father has given us to do, and to do it with the present sense that we are doing it for Him, and in his immediate presence. But this, once believed in, and taken with us into our work, instead of being a hindrance, would enable us to do it better than we could do without such a sense of his presence. It would make us calm, it would make us see more clearly all the bearings of what we were doing. It would take away the self-light which obscures, and give us instead God's light, wherein we see clearly. We must not, however, seek too high a link between our particular work and God's great purposes on earth. A man may have to drudge at a mechanical routine day after

day, week after week. His heart may at
times sink within him, not seeing any
bearing this routine has on the coming of
God's kingdom. But he ought not to
puzzle himself trying to find the link.
Enough if it is our Father's will for him.
Let him do it faithfully, in the full sense
that it is what God has given him to do, and
he need not seek to see more."

Again, in answer to a question, How is a
man to know for himself, or to satisfy another, that what he calls knowing God,
meeting with God, is not a delusion of his
own feelings, — how is he to be sure that he
has ever got beyond the circle of his own
subjectivity? — he first quoted the text,
" He that cometh unto God must believe
that He is, and that He is the rewarder
of them that diligently seek Him." And
then he went on to say that faith is itself,
to him who has it, its own evidence, and cannot be proved to be true by any extrinsic
evidence. He would have said, I suppose, to
him who doubts whether God can indeed
be met, Try it honestly, and you shall
know. He said, further, that in communion
with God we must not look for any sign, or
strong, vivid impressions borne in upon the

feelings, but must be contented with the quiet outgoings of faith, in the certainty it brings that it has an object which is real. More than this may be, often is, given, but this more is not necessary to a true faith.

He mentioned that once in recent years, after the death of his brother, when his whole body and mind were very much shattered, he found all the scaffolding of thoughts and arguments which he had laboriously built up fall away, and there was no help in them. What he might have offered to others at a like time were then wholly unavailing to himself. One thing only was helpful (and this, he said, was a precious lesson to him) : he had to begin at the old beginning, — he had to be just like a child, to believe, to put forth simple faith where he could see nothing, to roll himself over upon God. And this, I think he said, brought comfort when nothing else did.

At another time, while speaking on the subject, he said that he did not think the power of self-introspection, or the power of analysis, or the mental refinement which high education gives, were any help to realizing God, — rather perhaps hindrances.

He then spoke of a criticism of his own book on the Atonement, which had recently appeared in the " National Review." That criticism objected, among other things, that Mr. Campbell's view presupposed a realistic theory of Christ as containing all humanity in himself. Mr. Campbell did not feel this to be a weighty objection. For if we believe that all men live and have their being in God, and yet that their separate individuality remains intact, it is not more difficult to believe that Christ has in himself all humanity as its Root and its Head, without interfering with our separate and distinct individuality. Nor did he feel the force of another objection to his book in the same criticism, — that Christ could not repent, because repentance implies a personal sense of guilt. It is not, as the reviewer says, that Christ's repentance is made by Mr. Campbell to be the substitute for our repentance. His is not the substitute for ours, but the fountain of it. In Him, and in the light which He manifests of the Father's character and of our sin, only can we truly repent. " By the which will we are sanctified through the offering of the body of Jesus once for all." It is the will of the Father, which Jesus wholly met and fulfilled, which, entering into a man, and acquiesced in by him, made his own, really sanctifies him. But it can only enter into us, Mr. Campbell said, in and through the shedding of the blood of Jesus. " The wages of sin is death." This is the Father's irreversible way of looking at sin. He does not change this will. But Christ meets this will, says, " Thou art righteous, O Father, in thus judging sin ; and I accept thy judgment of it and meet it. I, in my humanity, say Amen to thy judgment of sin."

Then he added : " Those who, like Maurice, regard Christ's work as only taking away our alienation by making us see the Father's eternal good-will towards us, as this only and no more, they take no account of the sense of guilt in man. According to their view, there is nothing real in the nature of things answering to this sense of guilt. The sense of guilt becomes a mistake, which further knowledge removes. All sin is thus reduced to ignorance."

At another time, when speaking of Christ as the Head of humanity, I understood your father to say that he thought it one of Mr. Maurice's great dangers to carry this so far as to absorb in it all sense of our own individuality.

Lastly, recurring again to his book, and to the objection that it makes the Fatherly character overpower that of the Judge, he said that God could not be an all-wise and righteous Father if He did not judge. But he thought the Father came first in order of nature, just as the child loves his parent first, without knowing why or how. The gospel is before the law, as St. Paul shows, though the law comes in and has its place. As to Mr. Erskine's saying, " He judges only in order to save, to bring the soul to know its Father," he thought Mr. Erskine looked so entirely to the remoter end that he forgot the nearer. Mr. Campbell thought that God punishes, no doubt, to save and bring to the truth ; but He punishes also directly and immediately to testify his displeasure of sin. This is the main part of what I afterwards noted down of his conversation during that hour.

Of other times when I met and conversed with your father I have kept no record, and therefore cannot recall them now. But of a two days' visit he paid me at St. Andrews in July, 1868, I have a very distinct remembrance, though I took no notes of what he then said.   As we walked about during these two days, he talked of many things besides theology — indeed, he did not en- large on this subject, unless when ques- tioned, and this I did not then do.   I remem- ber his speaking of St. Columba with great interest, and quoting a Gaelic verse said to be by him.   I put it down at the time and have it somewhere.   What especially struck me of his conversation at that time was the extent to which, during recent years, he seemed to have opened his mind to subjects of general literature and philosophy.   In all his remarks on these, there was a weight and originality one seldom meets with, as of one who knew nothing of the common and wearisome hearsays that pass current among the so-called educated, but as if everything he uttered had passed through the strainers of his own thought, and came thence pure and direct.   Whatever he said bore the mint-mark of his own veracity, and commended itself as true, — true, that is, not only as regarded him, but true in itself.   All his judgments of things and of men, while they betokened that subtle and reflective analysis which belonged to him, had a scrupulous justness and exactness. Penetrating inwardness there was, and watchful conscientiousness of thought, but at the same time eminent sanity of judgment. Above all, you felt that all his thoughts and feelings breathed in an atmosphere of perfect charity.

One or two theological items I can still recall. Shortly before he left me, in speaking of his own book, he dwelt on the importance of that part of it which dwells on the retrospective aspect of the atonement. This aspect, he said, was in his view essential to the full truth of the doctrine. He spoke with regret of the fact that many who sympathized so far with his view had dropped this aspect out of sight, and had taken up solely what he says of the prospective aspect of the atonement. This I understood him to say was to misrepresent his position, and to give a quite inadequate view of the great subject. Owing to this one-sided representation of his view, it had come to pass that he had been identified with Maurice, which, if his book were fairly interpreted, he never could be. I inquired how far he agreed with the view which Mr. Erskine took of the relation of the Father and the Son, — the view which Mr. Erskine afterwards set forth in his last work, " The Spiritual Order." As far as I now remember he liked what was positive in the view, but thought it had a negative side which he could not agree with. He feared that in Mr. Erskine's view the personality of the Holy Spirit might be lost sight of; and from this he shrank.

These are the chief things I remember of that visit. You will not expect me to say anything of the impression left on me by your father's character. This only I may say, that like all who were admitted to know him, I felt then, as always, that he was one of the few men I have met who are truly described by the words " holy " and " saintly." A remark which Norman Macleod made about him in the funeral sermon he preached shortly after his death struck me at once as exactly expressing what I had often felt. It is that whenever you conversed with him alone, he made you feel that there was a Third Being there, in whose presence he distinctly felt himself to be. Norman wrote that sermon, I know, under much pressure of spirit, and as far as the wording goes, it is but a broken utterance. But it contained much of what lay nearest Norman's heart. In the last night I ever passed with him, he was full of your father, and what he had been to him. It was on the 18th of March, 1872, when we traveled together by the night mail train to London. Norman had been but a week or two before present at your father's funeral. He said in his own characteristic way that he had never before felt so thankful for the privilege of extempore prayer, as that, when called on to take part in the ceremonial in Rosneath Church, he could kneel down beside the coffin, and pour out his heart in thankfulness to God for all that your father had been to him.

He then talked long about him, and how much he had received from him during all those years from boyhood. He said that if he were asked to write your father's life, it would probably be the last thing he would ever write, and he would throw his whole heart into it, and try to make it the best. Before three months from that time were over, Norman was called to go where your father had just gone.

JOHN MACKINTOSH OF GEDDES.

[IN A LETTER TO NORMAN MACLEOD.]

IT is long since you asked me to write down my remembrances of John Mackintosh. I have long delayed, but shall do so no longer. Many of the times and scenes through which we passed together, the things we did, long talks we had, have already passed from my memory, but they have left behind a total impression which will not pass.

It was about the beginning of November, 1837, I think, on his first coming to Glasgow College, that we met and became acquainted. Years before, we had been at the Edinburgh Academy together, but as we were in different classes, we had not known each other to speak to. I knew him, however, by name and appearance, and seem now to see, as if it had been but yesterday, the two brothers, uniformly dressed in a suit of sky-blue from head to foot, sitting always together at the head of their class, — the

younger and smaller first, the elder next to
him. Though it is full twenty years since,
his appearance is clearly before me, and the
reputation that went with him, not only for
ability, but for character beyond his years.
There was about him even then a calm collected air, as of one who had a purpose before him and went straight to it, undisturbed by other aims. It may be that I
look back on that early time through the
light of what I afterwards knew ; but however this may be such it now appears in
retrospect.

The time when he entered Glasgow College was, as you will remember, a stirring
one in that University. Peel had been
elected Lord Rector the year before. The
Peel Club had been established to support
his principles ; political feeling, which was
then high among the students, added interest to life, and quickened the stir of thought.
But it is not as a young politician that we
think of him as he then was, but rather
as a chief favorite in that small circle of
friends, of which your father's hearth was
at that time the centre. There were in all
about ten or twelve of us between the ages of
sixteen and eighteen. Many of us had come

from the Edinburgh Academy; most were preparing for Oxford or Cambridge. We were then at that delightful time of life when the fresh heart of boyhood, first freed from restraint, leaps forward eagerly to the opening interests of manhood. Seldom do a band of friends live together on terms so happy, so intimate, so endearing, as those on which evening after evening we used to meet in that room in your father's house (known amongst us as the Coffee-room), or in the lodgings of some one of our number. Many interests there met and harmonized : poetry, philosophy, politics, or field-sports and other amusements. In these things, though John took some part, he was not ardent or conspicuous. Two things specially marked him. One was his scrupulous regularity in all things, and his conscientiousness in preparing each evening the college work of next day. In this he was a pattern to all of us, to which all did honor, whether they followed him or not. The other was the singleness of aim and resolute purpose with which he set his face toward divine truth, and to live an earnest religious life. This last I have heard of, but never saw equaled in a boy of his age. He used at

that time to attend the meetings of the College Missionary Society, and other things
of this kind, a practice in which, so far as
I knew, he was alone among the younger
students. But he was not remarkable for
any precocious activity, but rather for strict
self-discipline and thoroughness of purpose,
which made him, while earnestly seeking
the higher things, never neglect the lowest
duties. Mr. William Burns, who was then his
private tutor, greatly encouraged him in his
religious endeavors; and he used to know
and often to attend the church of Dr. Duncan. I ought perhaps to add, that these high
moral and religious qualities were at that
time not unaccompanied by a certain shade
of the austereness which some think characteristic of religious people in Scotland. But
however this may be, all his companions
felt the force of his goodness. Their great
love for him as a friend was mingled with
deep respect, I might almost say reverence,
for his whole character. Two sessions, two
most delightful winters, we were together
in Glasgow, and then came the 1st of May,
1839. On that day our band of friends
shook hands, and bade farewell to each
other. They went each on his separate

way, and never all met again, nor can meet now, any more in this world. It was indeed a golden fellowship, much to be remembered by all who shared it; and none did more to sanctify and endear it than he who was among the earliest taken.

After this, I have no distinct remembrance of our meeting till the midsummer of 1843. Then, after he had taken final leave of Cambridge, before returning to Scotland, he came to visit Oxford and some of his old Glasgow friends, who were undergraduates at Balliol College. It was then I heard from himself, and for the first time, that after long deliberation he had made up his mind to join the Free Kirk. Much had passed over both of us since we parted at Glasgow; and you can imagine how delightful it was, after so long an interval, to renew our old companionship. For several days we wandered together among the colleges and old gardens, and by the banks of the river; and the antique air of the place seemed greatly to impress him. He noticed, I remember, some difference between undergraduate life, as he had known it at Cambridge, and what he saw of it at Oxford; and seemed to think that we were

more intimate with the rest of our College
than he had been with the men of his.
This may have been owing to the difference
between a small college like Balliol, and
one so large as Trinity. At the same time,
my impression is that while there he had
lived a secluded life, chiefly with a few like-
minded friends, and never entered into the
main current of college society. He seemed
to think that it would have been otherwise
with him, if he had been at Balliol. It
might have been so, but of this I cannot
judge. "The Oxford movement" was then
at its height, and he took much interest in
all that he saw and heard regarding it. I
can remember standing with him in the
great square of Christ Church, to watch
Pusey's spare, bowed down, surpliced form,
as he returned from prayer in the Cathedral. He was present also in St. Mary's on
one of the last Sunday afternoons that Newman's voice was heard there or elsewhere as
a minister of the English Church. After a
few bright days we parted, and were never
again so long of meeting till he last went
abroad. One change, and only one, seemed
to have passed over him during our long
separation. The tinge of severity which I

was aware of formerly had wholly disappeared. Without losing his singleness or strength of purpose, he had grown, I thought, more gentle, more serene, more deeply loving towards all men. Every time we met, up to the last, this impression was confirmed.

From this time onward I had the great happiness of seeing a good deal of him, generally twice every year, at Christmas and at midsummer. He used sometimes to visit me at my home; but oftener I visited him in Edinburgh, or met him in your manse. During this time he was attending Dr. Chalmers' Divinity Lectures, visiting the poor in an old town district, teaching their children, and sometimes he attended some other of the professors. He was much taken up with Dr. Chalmers, and used to tell me much about him. He loved to dwell, too, on his little peculiarities, some of which greatly amused and delighted him. Our conversation during these times often turned on the things in which he was then engaged, — on the difference between English and Scottish universities, English and Scottish theology. About this time he read a good many of Newman's parochial sermons, and was

greatly struck by his wonderful power in
laying bare men's hidden character, and
putting his finger on the secret fault. Not
that he ever inclined towards the peculiar
doctrines of Newman, — from these, you
know, he was always far enough removed;
but this did not in the least hinder him from
freely opening his heart to these wonderful
writings, which for depth and inwardness
are perhaps unequaled in this century. I
did indeed admire his rare candor, which
was with him fully as much moral as intellectual. However widely a man differed
in opinion or sentiment from himself, it
seemed he did not care to dwell on the dif-
ferences, but rather to open his mind fairly
to take in whatever of good or true he had
to teach. This open-mindedness in one so
earnest and fixed in his own mind was very
remarkable; and the whole seemed so evenly
balanced that, while he was not only fair
but sympathetic towards all men, there appeared no symptom of that weakness and
uncertainty of thought often visible in those
whose sympathies are stronger than their
heads. Akin to this was his power of entering into works the ablest, and to many
men the most perplexing, without harm.

One summer, while he was in Edinburgh, I remember he went carefully through Kant's " Religion within the Limits of Reason." Few books, I imagine, would be more unsettling to most young men ; but though he read it with much attention, and seemed thoroughly to perceive its bearings, it did not seem to cast even a momentary cloud over his clear spirit. This may have been, in part, no doubt, because the turn of his mind was not speculative ; but much more, I believe, because religious faith was in him no longer matter of mere opinion and discussion, but rooted there, where no reasonings of men could shake it.

In those years, when I used to meet him in Edinburgh or elsewhere, there are some days which stand out with peculiar vividness in my memory. One summer he retired to Queensferry for a time, to combine more undisturbed study with pure air and a pleasant neighborhood. His days were there divided between his books and solitary walks among the woods and grounds of Hopetoun and Dalmeny, enjoying the grand views they command up the Forth to the Perthshire Highlands, and downward to the German Ocean. Twice I rode over

from Houston, and spent an afternoon with
him. One of these times he took me into
the park of Dalmeny, to a shady terrace,
which was a favorite haunt of his; and
there we walked up and down for long in
earnest talk. He then accompanied me for
some way on my road homeward. The
thought of that evening brings strongly to
mind the depth and tenderness of his sympathy for all his friends' anxieties, whether
outward or inward. In freeness it was liker
a woman's than a man's sympathy. And
there was a healing for the griefs of others
in the pureness of the mind that opened
to share them. Another time we met, and
whiled away part of a summer afternoon on
the high pastures of Midhope, looking over
the Firth of Forth. Then we made the
burn our guide, and let it lead us from the
open grass fields down through its deep
woody glen, past the antique house of Midhope, till it reaches the salt sea-water.
Tennyson was among our other thoughts
that day, and we chanted to each other that
beautiful melody of his, —

"Flow down, cold rivulet, to the sea —
Thy tribute wave deliver."

We knew not then how truly that burden applied :—

"No more by thee our steps shall be,
    Forever and forever."

But no shadow passed over that afternoon ;
it was altogether a bright one, and is as
bright in retrospect as it was when present.
Afterwards he wrote to me saying how
much he had enjoyed it, and inclosing some
feeling verses of his own. I would have
sent them to you, but I cannot now recover
them.

Those visits which I used to pay to you
twice yearly at Dalkeith Manse, were generally in company with John Mackintosh.
We went together and left together ; and as
we returned to Edinburgh, the feeling was
shared and expressed by both that there
were few things so full of refreshing as these
visits. One Sunday morning in winter, I
specially remember we had set our tryst at
a certain spot, a little way from Edinburgh,
whence we walked leisurely through by-
roads to Dalkeith. The morning was very
calm, and his spirit was in keeping with
the quiet of the time, and seemed to lead
others insensibly to share his own serenity.

It must have been one of our last times
of meeting that I went on a summer day
to find him in his lodgings, hoping to spend

some hours with him. He told me that he
was going that evening to the West Port,
to hear Dr. Chalmers speak to the working
people about the church which he was
building for them in the heart of that un-
sightly district. We went together through
lanes and closes, foul with all uncleanness,
till we found ourselves in the loft of a large
tannery. That low-roofed noisome loft was
crowded with the poorest inhabitants of that
poor neighborhood, who had come together
from their work or their garret just as they
were. At the head of the low-roofed dingy
room stood the venerable man, his hair
more white, and his body feebler than of
old, but with energy unabated, speaking to
these unlettered people not in his usual co-
pious eloquence, but with a direct homeli-
ness of speech, such as the poorest could understand. He told them how he had got that
church built, that others had subscribed
much, but that they must give some help
themselves; that others might well assist
them, but that they should not suffer everything to be done for them; that he would
not, even if he could, get the church completed, till they had given him each what
they could. From this he branched off to

speak of self-help in general, of masters and employers, adding maxims of thrift and practical political economy, moral advice, and religious exhortation, all naturally blended together, and all warmed by the most opened brotherly heart for those he was addressing. It was the last time I remember to have seen Dr. Chalmers, and one of the last surely that I was with John Mackintosh. After this I must have been with him at least once — the Christmas before he left Scotland. But I cannot recall anything special that then took place. Neither, strange to say, can I now remember the time of our last parting, so little thought had I that it was to be our last. When I heard that he was going abroad, I wrote to ask him to visit me here on his way. But soon I learned that he had gone to London by sea, on that continental tour from which he did not return.

ARTHUR HUGH CLOUGH.

It was towards the end of 1840 that I first saw A. H. Clough. As a freshman I looked with respect approaching to awe on the senior scholar, of whom I had heard so much, stepping out on Sunday mornings to read the first lesson in Balliol Chapel. How clearly I remember his massive figure, in scholar's surplice, standing before the brass eagle, and his deep feeling tones as he read some chapter from the Hebrew prophets. At that time he was the eldest, and every way the first, of a remarkable band of scholars. The younger undergraduates felt towards him a distant reverence, as a lofty and profound nature quite above themselves whom they could not quite make out, but who was sure to be some day great. Profaner spirits, nearer his own standing, sometimes made a joke of his then exceeding silence and reserve, and of his unworldly ways. But as he was out of college rooms and reading hard for his degree, we freshmen only heard of his reputation from a distance, and seldom came in contact with him.

It must have been early in 1841 that he first asked me to breakfast with him. He was then living in a small cottage, or cottage-like house, standing by itself, a little apart from Holywell. There he used to bathe every morning all the winter through, in the cold Holywell baths, and read hard all day. There were one or two other freshmen there at breakfast. If I remember right, none of the party were very talkative.

I have heard that about that time he wrote one day in fun an oracle, in the style of Herodotus, to his brother scholar, who was reading like himself for the Schools. The Greek I forget; the translation he sent with it ran something like this : —

> " Whereas, —— of Lancashire
>   Shall in the Schools preside,
> And Wynter to St. Mary's go
>   With the pokers by his side ;
> Two scholars there of Balliol,
>   Who on double firsts had reckoned,
> Between them two shall with much ado
>   Scarce get a double second."

This turned out only too true an oracle.

Since the beginning of class-lists the succession of firsts among Balliol scholars was
unbroken. And few Balliol scholars had
equaled, none ever surpassed, Clough's reputation. I well remember going, towards
the end of May or the beginning of June,
with one of the scholars of my own standing, to the school quadrangle to hear the
class - list read out, the first time I had
heard it. What was our surprise when the
list was read out, and neither of our
scholars appeared in the first class. We
rushed to Balliol and announced it to the
younger Fellows who were standing at
their open window. Many causes were
assigned at the time for this failure — some
in the examiners, some in Clough's then
state of spirits; but whatever the cause, I
think the result for some years shook faith
in firsts among Clough's contemporaries.
It made a great impression on others; on
himself, I fancy, it made but little. I
never heard him afterwards allude to it as a
thing of any consequence. He once told
me he was sick of contention for prizes and
honors before he left Rugby.

In the November of the same year he
tried for a Balliol Fellowship, but was not

successful. Tait, however, was strong in his favor, and, I believe, some other of the Fellows. I remember one of them telling me at the time that a character of Saul which Clough wrote in that examination was, I think he said, the best, most original thing he had ever seen written in any examination. But Oriel had at that time a way of finding out original genius better than either Balliol or the Schools. In the spring of 1842, Arthur Hugh Clough was elected Fellow of Oriel, the last examination, I believe, in which Newman took part. The announcement of that success I remember well. It was on the Friday morning of the Easter week of that year. The examination was finished on the Thursday evening. I had asked Clough and another friend, who was a candidate at the same time, to breakfast with me on the Friday morning, as their work was just over. Most of the scholars of the college were staying up and came to breakfast too. The party consisted of about a dozen. We had little notion that anything about the examination would be known so soon, and were all sitting quietly, having just finished breakfast, but not yet risen from the table. The door opened wide; entered a Fellow of another college, and, drawing himself up to his full height, he addressed the other candidate: "I am sorry to say you have not got it." Then, "Clough, you have;" and stepping forward into the middle of the room, held out his hand, with "Allow me to congratulate you." We were all so little thinking of the Fellowship, and so taken aback by this formal announcement, that it was some little time before we knew what it was all about. The first thing that recalled my presence of mind was seeing the delight on the face of Clough's younger brother, who was present.

In the summer of 1842, while I was reading in a retired part of Wales with two or three others, Clough, then wandering through the Welsh mountains, one morning looked in on us. I took a walk with him, and he at once led me up Moël Wyn, the highest mountain within reach. Two things I remember that day: one, that he spoke a good deal (for him) of Dr. Arnold, whose death had happened only a few weeks before; another, that a storm came down upon the mountain when we were half way up. In the midst of it we lay for some time close above a small mountain tarn and watched the storm-wind working on the face of the lake, tearing and torturing the water into most fantastic, almost ghostly shapes, the like of which I never saw before or since. These mountain sights, though he did not say much, he used to eye most observantly.

Early in the autumn of 1843, Clough came to Grasmere to read with a Balliol reading party, of which I was one. He was with us about six weeks, I think, staying till towards the end of September. This was his earliest long vacation party, all things on a smaller scale than his later ones by Loch Ness, or on Dee-side, but still very pleasant. He lived in a small lodging immediately to the west of Grasmere church; we in a farmhouse on the lake. During these weeks I read the Greek tragedians with him, and did Latin prose. His manner of translating, especially the Greek choruses, was quite peculiar; a quaint archaic style of language, keeping rigidly to the Greek order of the words, and so bringing out their expression better, more forcibly and poetically, than any other translations I had heard. When work was done

we used to walk in the afternoon with him
all over that delightful country. His "eye
to country" was wonderful. He knew the
whole lay of the different dales relatively to
each other ; every tarn, beck, and bend in
them. He used, if I remember right, to
draw pen-and-ink maps, showing us the
whole lineaments of the district. Without
any obtrusive enthusiasm, but in his own
quiet, manly way, he seemed as if he never
could get too much of it — never walk too
far or too often over it. Bathing, too,
formed one of his daily occupations, up in a
retired pool of the stream that afterwards
becomes the Rotha, as it comes out of
Easedale. One walk, our longest, was on a
Saturday, up Easedale, over the Raise by
Greenup, Borrowdale, Honister Crag, under
the starlight, to Buttermere. In the small
inn there we stayed all Sunday. Early on
Monday morning we walked, by two mountain passes, to a farm at the head of Wastwater to breakfast. On the way we crossed
Ennerdale, and up the pass close under the
nearly perpendicular precipices of the Pil-
lar — a tall mountain, which is the scene
of Wordsworth's pastoral of "The Brothers." From the head of Wastwater, up

past the great gorge of the Mickledoor, to
the top of Scawfell, then down past the
east side of Bowfell towards Langdale
Pikes, and so home to Grasmere. As we
passed under Bowfell a beautiful summer
afternoon, we lay a long time by the side
of the lovely Angle Tarn. The sun, just
before he sunk beside Bowfell, was shower-
ing down his light, which dimpled the
smooth face of the tarn like heavy drops of
sun-rain. Every now and then a slight
breeze would come and scatter the rays
broadcast over the little loch, as if some
unseen hand was sowing it with golden
grain. It was as memorable an appearance
as that different one we had seen a year
ago on Moël Wyn. These things, though
Clough observed closely, and took pleasure
in, he did not speak often about, much less
indulge in raptures.

Some of our party were very good hill-
men. One day, five or six in all set out on
a race from our door by Grasmere Lake to
the top of Fairfield. He was the second
to reach the summit. His action up-hill
was peculiar; he used to lay himself forward almost horizontally towards the slope,
and take very long strides, which carried

him quickly over the ground. Few men, so stout as he then was, could have matched him up a mountain.

Shortly after this time at Oxford, somewhere, that is, between 1843 and 1845, I remember to have heard him speak at a small debating society called the Decade, in which were discussed often graver subjects, and in a less popular way, than in the Union. Having been an unfrequent attender, I heard him only twice. But both times, what he said and the way he said it were so marked and weighty as to have stuck to memory when almost everything else then spoken had been forgotten. The first time was in the Oriel Common-room; the subject proposed — " That Tennyson was a greater poet than Wordsworth." This was one of the earliest expressions of that popularity — since become almost universal — which I remember. Clough spoke against the proposition, and stood up for Wordsworth's greatness with singular wisdom and moderation. He granted fully that Wordsworth was often prosy, that whole pages of the " Excursion " had better have been written in prose; but still, when he was at his best, he was much greater than any other modern English poet, saying his best things without knowing they were so good, and then drawling on into prosaic tediousness, without being aware where the inspiration failed and the prose began. In this kind of unconsciousness, I think he said, lay much of his power. One of the only other times I heard him speak was, about the same time, when a meeting of the Decade was held in Balliol Common-room. The subject of debate was — "That the character of a gentleman was, in the present day, made too much of." To understand the drift of this would require one to know how highly pleasant manners and a good exterior are rated at Oxford at all times, and to understand something of the peculiar mental atmosphere of Oxford at that time. Clough spoke neither for nor against the proposition; but for an hour and a half — well on two hours — he went into the origin of the ideal, historically tracing from mediæval times how much was implied originally in the notion of a " gentle knight " — truthfulness, consideration for others (even self-sacrifice), courtesy, and the power of giving outward expression to these moral qualities. From this high standard he traced the deterioration into the modern Brummagem pattern which gets the name. These truly gentlemen of old time had invented for themselves a whole economy of manners, which gave true expression to what was really in them, to the ideal in which they lived. Their manners, true in them, became false when adopted traditionally and copied from without by modern men placed in quite different circumstances, and living different lives. When the same qualities are in the hearts of men now, as truly as in the best of old time, they will fashion for themselves a new expression, a new economy of manners suitable to their place and time. But many men now, wholly devoid of the inward reality, yet catching at the reputation of it, adopt these old traditional ways of speaking and of bearing themselves, though they express nothing that is really in them.

One expression I remember he used, to illustrate the truth that where the true gentle spirit exists, it will express itself in its own rather than in the traditional way. " I have known peasant men and women in the humblest places, in whom dwelt these qualities as truly as they ever did in the best of lords and ladies, and who had invented for themselves a whole economy of manners to express them, who were very ‘poets of courtesy.’ ”

His manner of speaking was very characteristic, slow and deliberate, never attempting rhetorical flow, stopping at times to think the right thing, or to feel for the exactly fitting word, but with a depth of suggestiveness, a hold of reality, a poetry of thought, not found combined in any other Oxonian of our time.

It must have been in the autumn of 1845 that Clough and I first met in Scotland. One visit there to Walrond's family at Calder Park I especially remember. On a fine morning early in September, we started from Calder Park to drive to the Falls of Clyde. We were to spend the day at Milton Lockhart, and go on to Lanark in the evening. Besides Walrond and Clough, there were T. Arnold, E. Arnold, and myself. It was one of the loveliest September mornings that ever shone, and the drive lay through one of the most lovely regions in South Scotland, known as “ the Trough of Clyde.” The sky was bright blue, fleeced with whitest clouds. From Hamilton to Milton Lockhart, about ten miles, the road keeps

down in the hollow of the trough, near the
water, the banks covered with orchards,
full of heavy-laden apple and other fruit
trees bending down till they touched the
yellow corn that grew among them.   There
is a succession of fine country houses, with
lawns that slope towards lime trees that
bend over the river.   It was the first time
any of us but Walrond had been that way,
and in such a drive, under such a sky, you
may believe we were happy enough.   We
reached Milton Lockhart, a beautiful place,
built on a high grassy headland, beneath
and around which winds the Clyde.   Sir
Walter Scott, I believe, chose the site, and
none could be more beautifully chosen.   It
looks both ways, up and down the lovely
vale.

As we drove up, near ten o'clock, we
found the late Mr. J. G. Lockhart (Scott's
biographer) walking on the green terrace
that looks over the river.   The laird himself
being from home, his brother was our host.
Soon after we arrived, his daughter, then
very young, afterwards Mrs. Hope Scott,
came out on the terrace to say that breakfast was ready.   After breakfast she sang,
with great spirit and sweetness, several of

her grandfather's songs, copied into her mother's books by herself, when they were still newly composed. After listening to these for some time, her brother, Walter Scott Lockhart, then a youth of nineteen or so, and with a great likeness to the portraits of Sir Walter when a young man, was our guide to an old castle, situated on a bank of one of the small glens that come down to the Clyde from the west. It was the original of Scott's Tillietudlem in " Old Mortality." A beautiful walk thither; the castle large, roofless, and green with herbage and leafage. We stayed some time roaming over the green deserted place, then returned to a lunch, which was our dinner; more songs, and we then drove off late in the afternoon to the Falls of Clyde and Lanark for the night. It was a pleasant day. Clough enjoyed it much in his own quiet way, — quietly, yet so humanly interested in all he met. Many a joke he used to make about that day afterwards. Not he only, but all our entertainers of that day, Mr. J. G. Lockhart, his son and daughter, are now gone.

In the summer of 1847, Clough had a reading party at Drumnadrochet, in Glen

Urquhart, about two miles north from Loch
Ness, where, about the beginning of Au-
gust, I, along with T. Arnold and Walrond,
paid him a visit. Some of the incidents
and characters in " The Bothie " were taken
from that reading party, though its main
scenes and incidents lay in Braemar. One
anecdote I especially remember connected
with that visit. On our way to Drumnadrochet, T. Arnold and I had made a solitary walk together from the west end of
Loch Rannoch up to Loch Ericht, one of
the wildest, most unfrequented lochs in the
Highlands. All day we saw only one
house, till, late at night, we reached another on the side of the loch, about six
miles from Dalwhinnie. It was one of the
loveliest, most primitive places I ever saw,
even in the most out-of-the-way parts of
the Highlands. We told Clough of it, and
when his reading party was over, later in
the autumn, he went on our track. He
spent a night at the inn at the west end of
Loch Rannoch, called Tighalyne, where he
met with some of the incidents which appeared in " The Bothie." He also visited
the house by the side of Loch Ericht, a
small heather-thatched hut, occupied by one

of the foresters of the Ben-Aulder forest. He found one of the children lying sick of a fever, the father, I think, from home, and the mother without any medicines or other aid for her child. He immediately set off and walked to Fort William, about two days' journey from the place, but the nearest place where medicines and other supplies were to be had. These he got at Fort William, and returned on his two days' journey, and left them with the mother. He had four days' walk over a rough country, to bring medicines to this little child, and the people did not even know his name. On these occasions in Scotland, he told me that he used to tell the people he was a " Teacher," and they were at once at ease with him then. I doubt whether he ever mentioned this to any one but myself, and to me it only came out casually.

If I am not mistaken, it was from this place that he took the original name of what is now Tober-na-Vuolich. In this year he visited the West Highlands, and went through

" Lochaber, anon in Locheil, in Knoydart, Moydart, Morrer, Ardgower, and Ardnamurchan."

In the first edition this line was —

"Knoydart, Moydart, Croydart, Morrer, and Ardnamurchan."

But he discovered afterwards that Croydart was only the way that the Gael pro-
nounce what is spelt Knoydart. During
this wander he saw all the country about
Ben Nevis, westward to the Atlantic —

"Where the great peaks look abroad over Skye to the
westernmost Islands."

He walked " where pines are grand in Glen
Mally," and saw all the country which, in a
few lines here and there, he has pictured so
powerfully in " The Bothie." The expression about Ben Nevis, with the morning
sprinkling of snow on his shoulders, is absolutely true to reality.

In this expedition he came to Glenfinnan,
at the head of Loch Shiel, the place where
Prince Charles met the Highland clans, and
unfurled his standard. Here, there used to
stand a nice, quiet, little-frequented inn,
where one could live for weeks undisturbed.
But at the time when Clough reached it, a
great gathering was being held there. The
Queen had gone to Loch Laggan, and the
ships that escorted her to Fort William were
lying at the head of Loch Linnhe. McDon-
ald of Glen Aladale had invited all the
officers of these ships to have a day's deer-

stalking on his property of Glen Aladale, down the side of Loch Shiel, and to have a ball at the Glenfinnan Inn after their day's sport. Clough came in for the ball. It was a strange gathering — the English sailors, officers, a few Highland lairds, Highland farmers and shepherds, with their wives and daughters, were all met together at the ball. Clough and one of his reading party were invited to join the dance, and they danced Highland reels, and went through the festivities like natives. The uproar was immense, and the ludicrous scenes not few. He often used to speak of it afterwards as one of the motliest, drollest gatherings he had ever fallen in with.

Often afterwards he used to speak of his Scotch adventures with great heartiness. There was much in the ways of life he saw there that suited the simplicity of his nature. Even when Englishmen would laugh at the baldness of our Presbyterian services, he would defend them as better than English ritualism and formality.

[NOTE. — The reader will bear in mind that these reminiscences are merely fragments, contributed to the memoir which introduces *The Poems and Prose Remains of Arthur Hugh Clough.*]

www.ingramcontent.com/pod-product-compliance
Lightning Source LLC
Chambersburg PA
CBHW030821270326
41928CB00007B/837

* 9 7 8 3 7 4 4 6 9 2 7 0 0 *